RESET

RESET

Business and Society
in the New
Social Landscape

JAMES RUBIN and
BARIE CARMICHAEL

Columbia University Press
Publishers Since 1893
New York   Chichester, West Sussex
cup.columbia.edu
Copyright © 2018 Columbia University Press

Library of Congress Cataloging-in-Publication Data
Names: Rubin, James R., 1968- author. | Carmichael, Barie, author.
Title: Reset : business and society in the new social landscape /
James Rubin and Barie Carmichael.
Description: New York : Columbia University Press, [2017] |
Includes index.
Identifiers: LCCN 2017031578 (print) | LCCN 2017051062 (ebook) |
ISBN 9780231545907 | ISBN 9780231178242 (alk. paper)
Subjects: LCSH: Organizational change. | Industries—Social aspects.
Classification: LCC HD58.8 (ebook) | LCC HD58.8 .R825 2017
(print) | DDC 658.4/062—dc23
LC record available at https://lccn.loc.gov/2017031578

Columbia University Press books are printed on permanent
and durable acid-free paper.
Printed in the United States of America

Cover design: Noah Arlow

CONTENTS

FOREWORD

ROGER BOLTON

In *Reset*, James Rubin and Barie Carmichael crystallize the significance of megatrends converging into a profoundly new social ecosystem that is changing the public's view of the role of business in society. The informal social compact between business and society that was accepted in the twentieth century is no longer sufficient. The authors offer a penetrating analysis of the challenges corporations face today, tracing the converging trends in pop culture, workforce demographics, media, business reporting, and large-scale issues that have dramatically transformed the social landscape in which business governance, strategy, and communication now operate. The result is a dichotomy of declining trust *in* and rising expectations *of* business. Empowered by today's transformative level of instantaneous communication, an activist public exercises unprecedented pressure to hold corporations accountable for their behavior. Rubin and Carmichael document the global phenomenon of the public's growing expectation that business must not only mitigate its negative social impact, but also address pressing societal needs, made more urgent in an era when governments and political leaders have become unwilling or less able to serve the public good.

Since the beginning of the industrial revolution, public opinion has significantly shaped the sociopolitical environment in which ever-larger and more important corporations seek to operate. Arthur W. Page, considered to be the first senior corporate public relations executive, observed in a 1939 speech on industrial statesmanship, "All business begins with public permission and exists by public approval." He explained, "The public permission takes the form of charters, licenses and legal authorizations of one kind or another. Public approval is generally represented by reasonable profits, reasonable freedom of action and a few kind words. A lack of public approval is expressed in a good many ways—laws, regulations, commission rulings, investigations, public hostility and most vital of all, by a lack of patronage."[1]

During the twentieth century, Page's observation played out in several waves of government regulation in response to public concerns about and distrust of business, with antitrust regulation early in the century; a significant increase in government involvement in the economy through the New Deal following the Great Depression; and the environmental, health, and occupational safety laws in the sixties and seventies. As the century came to an end and a new one dawned, corporate scandals led to the Sarbanes-Oxley rules in 2002, and the global market crash led to the Dodd-Frank financial regulation in 2008.

Throughout the century, a debate about the responsibility of business to society raged, with some (notably Milton Friedman) arguing that business's only responsibility is to deliver a profit to its shareholders and others maintaining that business has a responsibility to create value for a broader set of stakeholders—including society at large. Throughout this period, as government regulation increased and the responsibility of business was debated, an informal social contract emerged between business and the public. Business was expected to produce quality products and services at reasonable prices, to provide steady employment in a healthy and safe environment, and to support community institutions.[2]

This insightful volume of analysis and recommendations arrives at a critical moment: Corporations the world over are struggling to understand and cope with the demise of the twentieth-century social compact; the risks associated with stakeholder activism; and the simultaneous rising demands and opportunities for business to create real economic and social value that goes beyond its traditional stakeholder group of shareowners, customers, and employees. The corporate social responsibility movement, which initially saw businesses seeking to conduct their affairs in socially responsible ways, is evolving into an era of conscious capitalism[3] or shared value,[4] in which businesses are expected to create not just customer and shareholder value, but societal value, as well.

After thoroughly and persuasively documenting the new social landscape for business, Rubin and Carmichael make a bold observation: success in this challenging environment requires businesses to reset the sweet spot. Historically, business success has "meant finding the sweet spot where a customer's unmet need and a product or service intersected." Today, they contend, success depends upon hitting a three-way intersection: "Delivering a product or service that meets a customer's needs through profitable business strategies that also benefit society." The breadth of that three-way intersection will vary, with benefit corporations or b-certified companies, for example, having a broader intersection than most. However, as *Reset* comprehensively argues, all businesses—from multinational corporations to small or medium-sized enterprises—are expected to think more broadly about the value they create that simultaneously benefits customers, shareowners, and society.

In addition to a web-enabled public and evolving customer preferences driving this change, the simultaneous retirement of baby boomers (ten thousand every day) and the arrival of a new generation of leaders who are more loyal to values than to an organization have combined to become a significant change catalyst. Competition to recruit and retain the next generation of employees has made the market for talent as powerful a change agent as the market for products.

Rubin and Carmichael demonstrate how corporate management can address this new landscape. Capturing the confluence of multiple streams of current business thinking—the authentic corporation, corporate character, shared value, conscious capitalism, shared advocacy—they offer a strategic framework that provides the historic and social context for today's headline business news, as evidenced by their many detailed, timely examples.

Corporate identity, for example, was once understood in business literature as a tactical exercise focused on brand standards and the corporate logo. Today, however, a company wishing to manage its identity must attend to its corporate character, which includes purpose, values, and culture, along with business model, strategy, and brand. All of these must be defined and aligned to create an authentic, compelling, and unique identity. A company's character, Rubin and Carmichael argue, is demonstrated by how it does business, with its employees and external stakeholders acting as its perpetual public auditors.

Rubin and Carmichael make a major contribution to the understanding of strategic corporate risk management by introducing the concept of inherent negatives—reputational risks that derive from the company's business model and which increase as the company grows. By proactively identifying and addressing these inherent negatives, a company can mitigate their potential impact and, potentially, strategically convert an inherent negative to a shared value and a platform for shared advocacy with its stakeholders.

The unique perspectives that Rubin and Carmichael bring to many of the concepts illuminated in *Reset* have their genesis in collaborative work done by the coauthors at the University of Virginia's Darden Graduate Business School. Both of the authors began their careers on an academic track in English literature before moving to business education (Rubin) and corporate communication (Carmichael).

Rubin dropped out of college to study the double bass with the principal bassist of the Metropolitan Opera Orchestra in New York; he also studied classical bass at Boston

Conservatory. He became one of the top jazz bassists in Boston, with regular gigs at places like the Parker House Hotel. In his late twenties, Rubin returned to college and obtained a BA in English literature from Boston University. He pursued a PhD in English at the University of Virginia, where he taught courses on Shakespeare, the English comic novel, and composition. In 1991, he joined the faculty at Darden.

Over twenty-five years of research and teaching management communication at Darden, Rubin created an incredibly rich volume of work that significantly advanced the understanding and teaching of corporate communication. His notes exploring the role of corporate communication in the enterprise read like a tutorial on the evolution of the strategic function and form the foundation of the thinking in *Reset*:

- Corporate identity and culture
- Changing contexts for reputation management
- Stakeholder engagement and the business model
- Corporate brand as social contract

Unlike many academic researchers and writers, Rubin's work was rooted in the practical reality of the practice of corporate communication. This made him a particularly valuable member of the Arthur W. Page Society, the global professional association of corporate chief communication officers, which he joined in 2002. Only a small number of elite academics are invited into membership of this prestigious organization. There, Rubin's unique personality made him a favored colleague for many.

I am well aware of Rubin's skill as a writer and teacher of cases as I had the rare honor of being the protagonist in a business case study that he wrote with Carmichael. I was invited by Rubin to teach the case with him on several occasions. Behind the self-deprecating façade of an absent-minded professor was an incredibly insightful mind whose observations and analysis delighted his students. Rubin was the first faculty recipient of the Frederick S. Morton Award, which annually recognizes a Darden student for excellence in leadership, along with the faculty member who contributed the most to that student's Darden experience. He was also a founding member of Blues Jam, a band composed of Darden faculty and students that played regularly at Darden events.

Rubin's partnership with Carmichael spanned more than a decade, including researching and copublishing articles and case studies as well as engaging with Darden MBA candidates in more than twenty class sessions. Their collaboration was anchored in Darden's Batten Fellows Program, which brings prominent thought leaders to collaborate with Darden faculty to contribute to knowledge on entrepreneurship, innovation, and business change.

Carmichael was named a Batten Fellow in 2005. Now a senior counselor at the global communications consultancy, APCO Worldwide, she brought more than thirty-five years of corporate communication experience to the fellowship, with positions including partner with the global advisory firm Brunswick Group and chief communication officer at Dow Corning Corporation, where her success in helping the company manage the reputational fallout from the silicone breast implant issue led the board of directors to elect her a corporate vice president and officer of the company.

Carmichael, a Page Society member since 1992, is known and respected by her peers as an expert in crisis communication and corporate reputation management. As Rubin discovered early in their collaboration, however, she also charted an unlikely path into business. Her first career choice was to teach English literature at the collegiate level. Graduating with honors from Carleton College, Carmichael's first career mentor, English Professor Harriet Sheridan, who would later become undergraduate dean of Brown University, recruited her return to Carleton to teach rhetoric and literature courses, sparking her interest in an academic track. After completing her MA at the University of Minnesota, Carmichael was invited to study in the PhD program. She had nearly completed her course work and begun her dissertation when she accepted a position in corporate communications.

Rubin's and Carmichael's common background in literature cemented their partnership and informed their thinking about strategic management communication. Their first co-authored article, which is cited in this book, "Oppositional Crises: A New Model for Crisis Management," was published in 2001. Rejecting the one-size-fits-all thinking that had then largely dominated the practice of crisis management as defined by the Johnson & Johnson Tylenol model, they advocated a structural analysis of a crisis. After discovering their joint admiration of influential literary critic Northrop Frye and his seminal *Anatomy of Criticism*, they applied Frye's literary genre analysis approach to business crises. Their article counseled that the structural differences in an oppositional crisis mandated business strategies that differed considerably from the Tylenol experience. Rubin and Carmichael continued to apply that same structural thinking to the focus of their Batten Fellowship Project, which introduced a new approach to corporate strategic risk management: inherent negatives as a basis for strategic business innovation. The impact of this collaboration is obvious in *Reset*.

Just days before Rubin's death in 2016, they had discussed his newly submitted manuscript and scheduled a call to review recent data relevant to the book from Darden's and APCO's Champion Brand research and strategic model. Due to Rubin's tragic accident, that call never happened, but Carmichael volunteered to prepare Rubin's first draft manuscript for publication.

What began as an editing process evolved to include development of substantive additional content, as new and highly relevant examples of business conduct occurred and were included. With Rubin remaining the lead author, Carmichael became a coauthor of the work.

Their shared love for literature, combined with Rubin's experience as a ground-breaking, practice-oriented researcher and thinker, and Carmichael's experience as a corporate reputation crisis expert and seasoned business leader, made this a magical combination. Having known and worked with both of them through our shared community in the Page Society, I am delighted to see this rich trove of analysis and inspiration, which is the culmination of their many years of collaboration.

EDITOR'S NOTE

After submitting the manuscript for *Reset* to Columbia University Press in June 2016, author James Rubin tragically died from complications following an accident. Barie Carmichael, Rubin's longtime collaborator and coauthor of several case studies with him, took on the role of coauthor and brought the book through to publication, adding relevant and updated material where appropriate. The Press wishes to express its gratitude to Carmichael for her contributions to this innovative work.

INTRODUCTION

When using the new (and brilliantly branded) Intel microchip in 1994, a Lynchburg College professor named Thomas Nicely found an error or "bug" in the processor's ability to correctly perform a complex calculation. Starting with an e-mail, this information went viral, as we would say today. Andy Grove, then Intel's CEO, at first dismissed the problem as irrelevant to consumers who were not conducting high-level mathematical research. The story then hit the *Wall Street Journal*, and Intel stock fell. At the time, Grove did not fully understand the implications of the new era of increased volume and speed for sharing information, which his chip had ironically enabled. Nor, from his perspective, was it immediately apparent that Intel had made an inherent promise to its stakeholders—that Intel chips are perfect. An offer to buy back the flawed computers resulted in a return rate of under 1 percent and restored Intel's share price. To describe his experience, Grove coined the phrase of a "strategic inflection point."[1]

The following year, Royal Dutch Shell found through scientific evidence that beaching an outdated oil rig, the Brent Spar, had no environmental advantages over sinking the rig in the North Sea. Greenpeace felt Shell's decision to sink the rig was unacceptable and sent inflatable boats carrying protesters to occupy the rig. Images of this encounter were posted on the web and made the front page of the *Financial Times*.

Neither corporation envisioned these scenarios. The velocity at which knowledge spread of the seemingly insignificant flaw in the Pentium chip stunned Intel. Similarly, Shell did not anticipate the effect that a relatively small nongovernmental organization would have on what was then the world's largest corporation. In 1995, compelling images of Greenpeace's protest were posted on the Internet in real time, making broadcast media's scheduled news cycle obsolete.

COMMUNITIES FORMING AT THE SPEED OF THOUGHT

Just over two decades later, we are at another "inflection point"—the new, perpetually evolving social landscape in which business must now operate. In an astonishingly short time, the volume of information now accessible on the Internet and social media platforms and the digitizing of all media (print and broadcast) has transformed how business engages its stakeholders, how stakeholders become engaged with corporations, and how business is perceived. More significantly, the collective impact of these changes is directly challenging how companies should be managed. To give some historical context on the speed of this change, it took radio thirty-eight years to reach fifty million users, a milestone television reached in thirteen years. Connections made in the new social landscape, however, have eclipsed those traditional measures of time. It took Facebook just three and a half years to reach fifty million users, while the "Draw Something" app got as many users within just fifty days.[2] Pokémon Go was launched on July 6, 2016. By September, the app had reached five hundred million downloads, with users walking nearly three billion miles with the app to catch its virtual creatures.[3]

Beyond the volume and speed of engagement, an equally important dimension has been the ability to quickly connect vast, like-minded communities of thought, with options to "like," "follow," or "block" quickly eliminating divergent points of view. The implications for business are profound. A raft of issues, once looming but seemingly intractable, have become matters of urgency: product safety, obesity and diabetes, the cost of health care and pharmaceuticals, environmental damage and global warming, and an already fragile trust in financial institutions, to begin by no means a comprehensive list. Today, the Internet, social media, and actively engaged stakeholders united in communities of thought, unbounded by the constraints of geography or time, are moving these issues from dormant to pressing, from intractable to demanding action. The result: an entirely new social landscape for business. Social media has made current affairs immediately accessible at any time in any location, enabling an unprecedented level of public engagement on today's most pressing issues. Millennials and Generation Z's, those born after 1996, may be the most publicly engaged generations in history. The Intel Pentium and Brent Spar crises, in retrospect, were early indicators of how web-enabled communities can affect business, hard to foresee at the time but now commonplace.

DECLINING TRUST AND RISING EXPECTATIONS

These rapid changes in technology and media have taken place against a backdrop of a steady decline of trust in business. Operating an organization in a low-trust environment is costly, requiring corporations to spend time and money to overcome initial skepticism about implementing new strategies or corporate branding campaigns or launching new products. When a company is distrusted, 57 percent of people surveyed believed negative information after hearing it once or twice, whereas 15 percent believed positive information. If a company is trusted, 51 percent believed positive information versus 25 percent believed negative information.[4]

Just as important, this decline of trust in business has coincided with a rise in the public's expectations that business should be responsible for many social issues now facing society, from obesity and food safety to global warming and pollution. Recognizing that businesses today must navigate a new social landscape, this book draws on research developed in a collaboration between the University of Virginia's Darden Graduate Business School and APCO Worldwide called Champion Brand that has tracked the views of over thirty-six thousand respondents on the relationships between business and society in fourteen of the world's largest economies. The 2014 results found that respondents exercise unprecedented scrutiny of and have expectations for corporations themselves and their behavior, not just their products. Among the research findings, 77 percent agreed that global corporations have a bigger impact on people's lives today than they did ten years ago, 60 percent agreed that companies now serve some functions in society that were previously reserved only for government, and 68 percent agreed that it is as important to know how a company operates as it is to know what it sells.[5]

The widening distance between declining trust and rising expectations creates a gap that corporations need to bridge in ever more inventive ways. In this new context, businesses can be swept up in fast-moving narratives, cast as the problem or solution, depending on their business strategies, policies, and actions. Or, they can find themselves a target in the political crossfire of the web's polarized communities. If management decides the gap between low trust and high expectations is not its business or ignores the potential business impact of the web's volatility, it risks the organization's ability to withstand the scrutiny of the new social landscape, at a time when global transparency is on the verge of a new inflection point, if not already a decided matter. Business, like politics, is no longer parlor sports taking place among gentlemen of influence and propriety behind the proverbial closed doors. Businesses, both their crises and brand-enhancing narratives, are now the staple of 24/7 cable news and social media. Baby boomers who are the first generation apt to rely more on their IRA or 401K stock portfolios in retirement than on their pensions (if they are among the minority who have them) or social security have a clear stake in how business more broadly operates.

How corporate management responds to the public's growing mandate may determine its very relevancy in this new social landscape.

A NEW CORPORATE PLAYBOOK

The digital revolution presents a pressing challenge for corporations, enabling them to positively engage in new ways but also providing global platforms for a web-empowered public to reveal and amplify their businesses' negative stakeholder impacts. The 2008 financial crisis cast risk in a new light as trust sank to new lows, and its legacy continues nearly a decade later for financial services companies. A particularly relevant cautionary tale is the role played by this new social landscape in BP's Deepwater Horizon crisis in 2010. Long before the spill, BP had followed the then well-established corporate playbook for advancing reputation and managing risk. On the upside, BP had invested in building its corporate brand, differentiating itself by claiming to be "beyond petroleum," positioned for the future by investing in alternative energy. To mitigate downside risk as a global energy company, BP also had the traditional crisis preparations in place: a dedicated crisis unit, practice drills, and recurring exercises involving hundreds of people to prepare for potential scenarios. What BP did not have in place was a YouTube channel, Facebook page, Flickr account, blog, or sufficient experience with Twitter.[6]

Yet by 2010, Facebook already had 608 million registered users, and Twitter had 26 million, growing to 150 million by 2011. The Deepwater Horizon disaster began on April 20, 2010. Clearly, the damage caused by a wellhead leaking fifty-three thousand barrels of oil per day is an unprecedented disaster. In that context, as BP has acknowledged, the only thing people want to hear is how the problem is being fixed. However, in the context of the new social landscape, BP accelerated their reputational damage by not taking part in social media conversations until launching their social media platforms on May 1, nearly two weeks after the rig exploded. In the warp speed of social media, that was a millennium. By mid-May, 2010, a fake BP Twitter account satirizing BP's corporate statements had twice the number of followers as the real BP account.[7] Even in 2016, as this book was being written, a June 2010 YouTube parody of the Deepwater Horizon disaster simulated by spilling coffee during a corporate meeting had over 13 million views and counting. The professionally produced skit features Kate McKinnon of *Saturday Night Live* and a cameo from Kevin Costner.[8]

Clearly, we are not in Kansas anymore.

Building a sustainable business in this new landscape requires more than memorable brand taglines and crisis preparation drills. Instead, the new landscape is fundamentally resetting the relationship between business and society, requiring strategic management solutions anchored in a critical outside-in understanding of the stakeholder footprint of the business model itself. Recent advances in corporate social responsibility are symptomatic of the fundamental changes at play, as companies make tactical adjustments to the stakeholder impact of their products' lifecycle supply chains. However, these changes are often individual initiatives rather than strategic changes in the way a business operates. The unprecedented global visibility and scrutiny of the corporation itself, not simply its products—from its governance and policies to its value proposition as an enterprise—are now driving stakeholder activism.

This book, rather than simply flagging the long-standing problems posed by declining trust, focuses on how corporate management can address the growing public mandate of the new social landscape to close the widening gap between eroding trust in and rising expectations for business.

NAVIGATING THE NEW SOCIAL LANDSCAPE

This book uses a set of central examples based on corporate case study field research on companies such as Aetna, the Coca-Cola Company, Nissan, Novo Nordisk, and UPS. This does not mean the format of this book is a casebook with framing. It does mean a section of each chapter will include examples illustrating the real-world implementation of the ideas we propose. Other examples will be used when they best illustrate a given point.

The first two chapters are introductory in the sense of framing the problem and raising questions. Chapter 1 describes the widening gap between the public's declining trust in business and its escalating expectations for business to address societal needs. The chapter briefly traces the causes of the phenomenon in terms of changes in media and technology, public opinion, and perception, creating a new social landscape that has reset the relationship between business and society. The second chapter provides an overview of the business strategies needed to close the trust-expectations gap, including a strategic frame to align business operations, policies, and governance with stakeholder expectations to mitigate risk and build the business. In this new era, web-enabled stakeholders are committed to holding business accountable for its behavior. Conducting business as usual in this changed landscape poses considerable risks.

Chapter 3 introduces the concept of inherent negatives, the latent negative stakeholder impacts inherent to a business model that increase as the company grows, magnifying the company's risk profile. As expectations for business increase and trust diminishes, companies that anticipate and proactively mitigate their inherent negatives as a way of doing business are better positioned to preserve their license to operate and grow. The chapter also discusses the co-dependency of risk mitigation and brand building. As risk is sufficiently mitigated, upside reputation and brand building may become new forms of value creation, including shared advocacy with key stakeholders and creating shared value.

Chapter 4 argues that the new landscape in which business is now conducted has reset the social contract for what is acceptable corporate character, with continuous internal and external stakeholder scrutiny. To withstand that always-on scrutiny, a company proves its character through its actions, through its behavior at all levels of stakeholder engagement that is consistent with its vision and values and for some companies, with its heritage. The importance of corporate character in this new era has repositioned the central role of employees whose status had eroded after years of vanishing manufacturing jobs at one end and "employees at will" at the other. With baby boomers retiring at a quickening rate, acceptable corporate character has become an essential attribute to attract and retain the next generation of leaders who expect that the words "We care about our people" have meaning.

SHIFTING SPOTLIGHT

Chapter 5 takes up the ways in which corporate branding is almost ubiquitous, not just in marketing but in expressing corporate character. Rising expectations for the role of business to address social needs has shifted the spotlight to the company behind the products and services it offers. The corporate narrative is no longer the exclusive domain of the company or its marketing initiatives. Instead, the power to shape the corporate narrative has shifted to stakeholders and perpetually evolving communities of thought on the Internet and social media. In this new landscape, stakeholders have evolved from consumers of information to creators and movers of information. It is difficult to imagine that just a decade ago, brand was considered securely in the product marketing function and corporate branding was considered by management academics as irrelevant. In the new social landscape, corporate brand when fully integrated with an organization's corporate character has become an essential differentiator.

Chapter 6 focuses on reputations lost and found, suggesting fundamental strategies to rebuild trust. In addition to expanding levels of transparency, the new landscape has exponentially compressed the time for an issue to gain critical mass and has given companies new tools to quickly address the situation. We present two case studies, Aetna and Dow Corning, that provide in-depth insights into their executive management teams' strategies central to restoring their reputations, with the lessons learned directly relevant to the long and costly road to restoring reputation. It should be no surprise that the process for restoring trust is like the process for building it at the outset, but the costs are higher and the time protracted.

Chapter 7 examines the implications of the book's overarching themes. Declining public trust and increasing public expectations for business's role in society have coincided with the rise of the public's voice, linking globally diverse stakeholders united by common interests to passionately advocate their concerns. This unprecedented environment for business requires new leadership skills for CEOs and their management teams to understand their business model— its inherent negatives and potential for shared advocacy and shared value—through the outside-in lens of their stakeholders. Companies who have embraced this new way of doing business are joining with stakeholders to discover mutually beneficial solutions to pressing issues, solutions that demonstrate the enlightened self-interests of *both* business *and* society.

Rather than philanthropy, business has a direct stake in a stable society with institutions that predictably work. Business cannot succeed in a failed society.

1

THE BUSINESS
TRUST-EXPECTATIONS GAP

I t should be no surprise to anyone that the public's trust in business has substantially eroded. Since 2006, the Gallup World Poll, interviewing more than 100,000 households in over 150 countries, has tracked an overall decline in confidence in public institutions, with the most dramatic declines in trust being found in financial institutions and national governments following the 2008 financial crisis. In the United States, Gallup has tracked decades-long declines in Americans' confidence in institutions.[1]

Whereas declining trust is old news, particularly for government and business, more significant is the concurrent increase in the public's expectations of corporations on a global scale. This widening gap between falling trust and increasing expectations for big business coincides with both the rise of corporate social responsibility and the astonishing rapidity of new and social media as becoming both productive and disruptive factors.

This chapter reviews how the gap between low trust and high expectations has evolved and reset in the relationship between business and society. Understanding that reset starts with an understanding of the context, dynamics, and magnitude of the dramatic changes that have occurred in the past thirty years. For current business leaders, this is a refresher course. For the next generation of business leaders, this provides important historical context.

RISING EXPECTATIONS FOR A BOTTOM FEEDER

The data for declining trust in big business are unequivocal. For the past decade, big business has been a bottom feeder among institutions in Gallup's long-established U.S. public opinion tracking study, with only Congress's abysmal performance displacing big business's lock on a last-place finish in 2008. In their race to the bottom, neither business nor Congress has scored more than a single-digit percent score for those declaring a "great deal" of confidence. Among all institutions tracked over the last decade—including often disparaged institutions like banks, organized labor, television news, and newspapers—Congress and big business have consistently ranked at the bottom.

Despite recent optimism based on the recovery of capital markets and corporate profits, the developed world has not fully recovered from its last asset bubble, as evidenced by stubbornly resistant pockets of low employment and still fragile consumer confidence. In the case of the United States, some level of distrust in big business and government has always been part of the "exceptional" individualistic American character.

The decline of public trust in large organizations over the past forty years began during the 1970s with Vietnam and Watergate, as Americans began to more widely question their institutions in new ways. Even in those divisive times, however, the media channels of network television, radio, and national newspapers built a national "consensus" and increasingly brought public attention to the events that shook their audiences' beliefs in institutions, as viewers, listeners, and readers shared unfolding events through a limited number of news sources. Today, "mainstream," or "establishment," media are themselves among the trust casualties, with a fragmented public now individually consuming or streaming their increasingly polarized sources of information. In this dramatically changed context, individuals on all sides of an issue become hardened in their own opinions reinforced by self-selected facts and stereotypes. The dynamics at play in the 2016 U.S. presidential election and the United Kingdom's "Brexit" vote were real-time exhibits of the often unpredictable consequences of these factors coming together to create a pervasive trust deficit.

Important nuance lurks, however, beneath the top-line data on trust in business. In Gallup's 2016 survey, confidence in small business was second only to confidence in the military for the most favorable ranking, with 68 percent declaring a great deal or quite a lot of confidence in small business.[2] Similarly, the Public Affairs Council's Pulse Survey results for 2011 to 2015 consistently differentiated between large and small business, with favorability for small business outscoring big business by a factor of more than 3 each year. The primary factor driving these diverging opinions on business?

Personal experience gained through direct engagement as a customer or an employee.[3]

Despite the dismal trust factor for major businesses, high expectations abound for the role of business in society. In the United States, findings from the 2015 Public Affairs Pulse Survey show that Americans expect positive social contributions from the business sector: protecting the environment (93 percent), contributing to charities (88 percent), and leading change to help society in ways that go beyond business (85 percent).[4] Similarly, in the Champion Brand study of fourteen of the world's largest economies, an overwhelming majority of the more than 36,000 respondents—94 percent—said that companies have the ability to shape a better society, and 73 percent reported believing that public scrutiny of corporate actions has increased in the past ten years.[5]

Even more significant for business, the public have become active information seekers to drive their expectations for business and act on them. In the global Champion Brand study, a large majority of respondents had, in the past month, gotten information on corporations through newspapers and online via websites or social media platforms. Astoundingly, almost three-quarters had converted that information to action in the past twelve months—most often in the form of initiating a conversation with friends or family about a company. However, large numbers also reported having changed their purchasing behavior because of their view of a company's practices or having influenced others to take or not take a job because of a company's social responsibility, environmental, or human rights policies or activities.

This degree of activism was substantial across all global markets, and, perhaps surprisingly, activism was markedly higher in Brazil, China, and India than in Canada, the United States, and Western Europe.[6]

NEW ERA OF BOTH/AND BUSINESS STRATEGIES

For business, the impact of this increasing gap between low trust and high expectations and the activism associated with it is profound, requiring more than a tweak in corporate taglines. Contrast previous CEO Jack Welch's General Electric with CEO Jeff Immelt's. Welch's focus on streamlining delivered steady returns to shareholders as he sought to grow fast in a slow-growth economy by being either number 1 or 2 in an industry or leaving it. In stark contrast, Immelt has declared that the purpose of General Electric is to grow its business while also solving pressing social issues through innovation. More than a tagline, "ecomagination" is a new strategy for GE:

> Ecomagination is GE's growth strategy to enhance resource productivity and reduce environmental impact at a global scale through commercial solutions for our customers and through our own operations. As part of this strategy, we are investing in cleaner technology and business innovation, developing solutions to enable economic growth while avoiding emissions and reducing water consumption, committing to reduce the environmental impact in our own operations, developing strategic partnerships to solve some

of the toughest environmental challenges at scale to create a cleaner, faster, smarter tomorrow.[7]

Both Welch and Immelt articulate growth strategies for GE, but the contrast in their approaches to how that growth is to be achieved represents a fundamental shift from an "either/or" to a "both/and" business paradigm. Welch's GE reflects a once-enshrined business dogma: Delivering an acceptable financial return to investors and stockholders is the exclusive, driving mandate for business, with any tradeoff favoring those financial stakeholders over any others. When a tradeoff is not a factor, excess profits can be applied to philanthropy or community relations as ancillary initiatives to the core mission of delivering a financial return to investors, with societal benefits being a positive, but indirect, result of GE's growth. Immelt's GE seeks strategies that, at their core, both grow the business and benefit society. It is not a zero-sum game with an "either/or" tradeoff. It is "both/and" through proactively seeking business strategies that directly benefit both investors and society.

This contrast is not unique to GE. It represents a dramatically changed context in which business governance, strategies, and communications now operate. We suggest that the "trust–expectations gap" is a culmination of years of growing public awareness about social issues from events such as the collapse of asset bubbles, to concerns over climate change, and more recently to issues such as obesity and product safety.

In parallel with this growing awareness of issues is the dramatic transformation in the fundamental concept of what is understood as "media," producing verbal gymnastics in trying to distinguish "media" from "mainstream" media, from "establishment" media, and now from "social" media, each with its own unique definition depending on who is speaking. Just as transformational has been the way information is now consumed, depending on one's generation, preferred device(s), mobility, and even current mood. Information consumption has become such an individual experience that many have wondered about the potential impact of an erosion of the social skills needed for real-world interpersonal relations and the ease with which stereotypes can thrive in the absence of direct contact with real people who can disrupt those stereotypes. For corporations, the consequence is not simply low trust but the combined impact of low trust and high expectations now playing out in a landscape that has revolutionized the basic elements of communications. Who is communicating about what, where, when, why, and how—the basic five Ws and one H—can be both transparent and unverifiable at the same time.

LOVE/HATE RELATIONSHIP

John Kenneth Galbraith, always a staunch and liberal Keynesian, argued that postwar prosperity, and indeed the American economy, worked through a system of checks and balances where government regulation checked business excesses, labor unions protected employees, and business stuck to its task of creating wealth through increased profit. Today, the steady decline in regulation and union membership that began with the Carter administration, accelerated under Reagan, and continued through Clinton with such innovations as the repeal of the Glass–Steagall Act, has blunted Galbraith's checks and balances.

Distrust and skepticism of commerce and industrialization have been contentious from the time of Shakespeare's *The Merchant of Venice* through Dickens's *Hard Times*, mercantilism, and the Industrial Revolution. Despite this skepticism, the public's heightened expectations for business to solve societal problems when combined with its sharp declining trust creates a love–hate relationship: We are suspicious of large corporations but expect the next Bill Gates or Apple to lead us out of a sluggish economy and back to prosperity. We elect Donald Trump as president of the United States based on both our anger at big business for abandoning the middle class and our hope that President Trump's business acumen can restore middle-class prosperity. De Tocqueville's prescient observation of the nineteenth century's potential conflict between individualistic equality and an obsession with business remains very much at play.

Business is far less beset by the unrealistic demands of the public, corporate critics, and nongovernmental organizations than it is a victim of its own success, of increasingly winning the argument that business can regulate itself and cure social ills, an argument that has taken thirty years to win a majority view.

Adding to the complexity has been the rise of large-scale "issues" attributed to the impact of business on society that have affected populations as a whole and helped create a background of anxiety and suspicion. In addition to affecting a given corporation, almost every industry has, along with a new set of high expectations, a set of issues that have proven difficult to solve. For consumer packaged goods, for example, there is the issue of general health and obesity, which has accelerated rapidly in the last few years; for pharmaceuticals, the issue has been cost and equitable access to medications; and for energy companies, there is pollution and global warming, which can be finessed only as long as global warming does not compromise business models and is positioned as simply a debate, rather than a scientific consensus on a potential calamity.

The gaps between declining trust and escalating stakeholder expectations for business, between these intractable issues and the ability to address them, have today met a transformative level of instantaneous communication enabled through unlimited access to the Internet, social media, and a world of screens.

THE LEGACY OF LOW TRUST

Since trust is so fundamental to transacting business on any scale, the mandate for business to recognize the impacts of the new landscape should be obvious. The impact of diminished trust for the nuclear energy industry is a classic example. Prior to the financial crisis of 2008, the energy industry in the United States had hoped to build up to thirty nuclear power plants, with some unlikely allies in the environmental movement seeing nuclear power as a cleaner alternative to fossil fuels, and President Obama mentioning nuclear power as part of a sustainable energy mix. At least in the United States, however, to date no sustained industry-wide communications campaign has been directed to the general public to make the case for building new and safer nuclear plants, even though no new plants have been brought online since 1979, following the partial nuclear meltdown at Three Mile Island. Japan's Fukushima nuclear disaster of 2011 was likely a serious setback for a renewed vision of new nuclear power plants safely dotting the American landscape, since the consequences of that disaster were all too immediate. The more severe consequences of climate change, for which nuclear power can be part of the solution, are relegated to a future date that has not yet arrived—even if many of the consequences have in fact already begun. Still, plausible arguments can be made on both sides of the argument over whether to build new nuclear power plants in the United States. Plainly the French have accepted this kind of energy production. But nearly forty years after Three Mile Island, the arguments in favor of nuclear power have been unable to overcome the legacy of lost trust and the concomitant resistance to nuclear power in the United States, and no concerted, sustained industry effort to engage the American public has taken place.

While operating a business during a low-trust period has become in some ways an accepted part of the background in our society, it nevertheless remains a significant hurdle for a company wishing to convey its message to a jaded public, build positive perceptions, or reposition itself. Advertisements showing a farmer in work clothes extolling the benefits of natural gas are less an attempt to convince viewers to sell the drilling rights to their properties than an effort to level the playing field of public opinion. The objective is to convert a negative public perception into a neutral one. Once neutrality is achieved, initiatives to build positive associations and sway public opinion to a favorable perception can be more effective.

The American Plastics Council ads of the recent, but less complex, decade of the 1990s showed a successful effort toward mitigating the famously negative connotation of plastics, still reeling three decades later from a single word—"Plastics"—whispered in the ear of Benjamin Braddock, portrayed by Dustin Hoffman in the 1967 film *The Graduate*. In response to the notion that paper was more readily recyclable, McDonald's made the highly visible decision in 1990 to abandon the plastic clamshell container for paper bags. The paper bags had to be lined with plastic to protect customers from greasy french fries and burgers thus confounding a real commitment to taking a side in the ongoing paper versus plastics debate we encounter nearly every time we make a purchase. Nevertheless, McDonald's decision made the need to mitigate public resistance to plastics more pressing. In response, the American Plastics Council funded an advertising campaign showing familiar everyday essentials—like a half gallon of milk—and explained that plastics made everyday conveniences possible and were no harder to recycle than other types of containers.

BP ads depicting happy residents of the Gulf of Mexico indirectly promote BP's commitment to the region in an attempt to mitigate negative perceptions following the Deepwater Horizon oil spill of 2010 and enable a rebuilding of so much lost reputation. BP may not be beyond redemption in their industry. The company has had substantial assistance from the region's trial lawyers' associations—although casting blame on an entity such as trial lawyers, however well deserved, tends not to work. News coverage claimed that BP, by cutting out middlemen in paying damages, ran afoul of local trial lawyers who felt left out of the perceived bonanza. BP countered the trial bar criticisms with full-page ads in national newspapers arguing for fair play. If anything can turn opinion toward an oil company, it is seeing them as victims of trial lawyers.[8]

In all these examples, corporations and industries have recognized the need to invest in rebuilding trust when unmet public expectations have stymied business goals. If managers simply accept the disparity between current levels of trust and rising expectations as the "new normal," restoring trust and engaging stakeholders will remain an uphill struggle. More and more effort must go into simply creating a level playing field. Apart from companies like BP that are rebuilding after a company-specific crisis, today business in general is starting out at a deficit with the public.

"DID YOU REALLY THINK YOU COULD BEAT GENERAL MOTORS?"

To understand the profound change this new social landscape represents for conducting business, it is good to recall——or to inform, in the case of digital natives and Generation Z's—how dramatically this context differs from the trust, shared expectations, and aspirations characteristic of not too distant past eras. These changes have fundamentally reset the social contract between business and society and the nature of the corporate brand promise.

There is a scene in the television series *Band of Brothers*, set in World War II, based on the book by Stephen Ambrose, that captures a previous era: GIs in Holland riding on trucks past lines of defeated Germans ask, "Did you really think you could beat General Motors?" These were the soldiers who came home to the GI Bill and a period of prosperity that would last into the 1970s. The first college graduate in a family could become a manager at a company like Kodak and spend his career, and secure retirement, in Rochester, New York. So, too, great American companies like Ford and IBM could provide the foundation for life-long careers, and managers (who were likely male, given the era) were not only Madison Avenue's "mad men" but also "car men" and "engineers" who "brought good things to life."

As Douglas Holt remarks in *How Brands Become Icons*, to become iconic a brand must interact with the larger culture in a way that is relevant to significant tensions or change in society. GE's advertisements for dishwashers and washing machines claimed that the head of the family and member of a growing middle class could save his wife from drudgery through its products and enjoy the fruits of prosperity even if he was not yet in a junior manager position.

Suburban houses rose in value. The Dow Jones annualized return was more than 10 percent. Average people owned homes and bought a new Ford or Chevrolet every few years or, if fortunate, moved up from a Bel Air to an Impala and possibly to a Cadillac. To be sure, the 1950s had its critics, as exemplified by novels like Sloan Wilson's *The Man in the Gray Flannel Suit*. Yet, compared to the Great Depression and the recent disruptions of globalization and asset bubbles followed by recessions, business was the engine of prosperity. For most, the management of big business took place somewhere outside their everyday lives in a place more rarified than the front page of the newspaper.

To be sure, this portrait has attained the status of nostalgia with all its capacity for oversimplification. Still, we can look at some examples from popular culture as a kind of shorthand to demonstrate the seismic shift in popular attitudes toward business.

The musical of 1961 and film of 1967 *How to Succeed in Business Without Really Trying* was conceptually a spoof on a self-help book of the same name and was the 1960s version of a genre that has been integral to the American psyche since Ben Franklin and Horatio Alger. The hero does succeed in business through reading the book but also through sheer self-confidence (no small thing today) and the help of the chief executive's secretary. The chief executive, Mr. Biggley, and his executives think the company makes widgets but are not sure. If a spoof of corporate office politics, it is a gentle spoofing where everyone is in on the joke.

While books and films like *The Man in the Gray Flannel Suit* critiqued 1950s and 1960s conformity, they were more stories of individual angst than an indictment of the era's business and advertising, through which the characters in the retro television series *Mad Men* romp and wink at the notion that the first masters of the universe could sell anything.

Placed in context of the 1960s, these books, films, and shows were staged in the middle of a general prosperity that lasted from the end of World War II to a period of growing anxiety that began to take its contemporary form with the 1980s savings and loan crisis.

By 1987, the film *Wall Street* provided a dark and cynical exposition of insider trading, which foreshadowed later business scandals. The film features a plainly Faustian motif in which the main character, Gordon Gekko portrayed by Michael Douglas, saves his soul in the nick of time.

By the time of Paramount's 2015 film *The Big Short*, the gradually darkening view of business had progressed beyond the indictment of an individual villain tycoon like Gordon Gekko to an indictment of the whole financial services industry. In addition to tutoring viewers on the intricate financial instruments that caused the collapse of financial markets in 2008, *The Big Short* shows the unmitigated greed of those engaged with profiting from a gamed system. Its epilogue details the profits they achieved without personal consequence. No last minute soul saving in this quasi-docudrama. Interspersed throughout the movie are scenes of the public oblivious to what is going to happen to them amid their obsessions with iPhones and pop culture icons like the Kardashians.

PRIMETIME WORTHY

In addition to the dramatic changes in the way business is portrayed in pop culture, today the way media reports news about business has dramatically changed. Business news today is reported in "real time," dramatically changing the way the public, who today relies less on social security and more on a rising stock market to increase an IRA or 401K nest egg, stays informed. The wired world has made the twelve-hour, and even the twenty-four-hour, news cycle seem quaint. The speed of this change is astounding. It was not long ago that print journalism still led television and cable news. The decline of newspapers and the rise of online journalism has changed this mix. The *Wall Street Journal* provided some of the most penetrating investigative journalism into the financial crash of 2008. However, just eight years later by 2016, according to the Pew Research Center, the majority of American adults, 62 percent, were getting their news through social media, with Facebook, Reddit, and Twitter being the leading sources.[9]

For young managers or even journalists who rely on social media for news, mid-twentieth-century media may now be an historical anecdote; yet an understanding of the dramatic changes in media is crucial to understanding the implications of the gap between the low trust in and high expectations of business.

Put briefly, during that earlier era, the United States had three major networks—ABC, CBS, and NBC—broadcasting over the airwaves. In exchange for access to the airwaves, which were considered public property, the Federal Communications Commission (FCC) required public service programming which included, remarkable as it may seem to some today, some children's programming—hence *Romper Room*, an opportunity for a Baltimore entrepreneur whose wife taught school. (Many a fortune has been made by keeping an eye on FCC regulations.) Alongside the three

networks were the flagship newspapers of mostly major cities, the *Boston Globe, Chicago Tribune, Los Angeles Times,
New York Times, Washington Post,* and *Wall Street Journal*
being notable examples. Again, while editorial pages might
have slanted toward one or the other political party, and
tabloids thrived, there was in major newspapers, to use the
accepted expression, a "firewall" between editorial com-
ment and reporting, as well as one between business interests
and journalism.

Not long ago, business news had to reach a fairly high
threshold—say, the Union Carbide disaster in Bhopal—to
make it as news beyond the stock market pages. Indeed, the
primary function of newspaper stock market listings was
analogous to that of baseball box scores, with many middle-
class citizens prospering in the ever-rising market. Con-
glomerates with multiple and diversified business units like
Emerson, GE, and United Technologies acted like mutual
funds before mutual funds, and "blue chips" like Coca-Cola,
IBM, and Procter and Gamble did not lose money—one
hoped they were snug in one's grandmother's safety deposit
box. We can also draw a contrast between the discretion of
the press corps in this era and its omission of JFK's infideli-
ties versus the media's handling of Monica Lewinsky's unfortunate navy dress. That is, the ins and outs of news were once
handled with discretion; corporations and government officials made decisions somewhere beyond the everyday.

A significant inflection point for media and business was
the rise of cable television. While the technology was available in 1948 (just as television had been possible in the 1920s),
a reasonable date to consider in terms of its influence is

Ted Turner's founding of CNN in 1980. By 2006, 58 percent of American homes had cable subscriptions (this figure omits satellite connections). With the ever-expanding number of cable news channels came the demand for content, ushering in not only cable business news shows but also cable business networks.

Cable's growth became a significant factor in broadcast networks' quest for the sensational, or at least a more viewer-friendly, entertainment-leaning news format, triggering critics to bemoan competition's weakening of the wall between business and journalism. For our purposes, cable programming's hunger for content and the proven viability of business news as content migrated both to networks and newspapers.

To borrow a *Seinfeld* expression, business news was now primetime worthy. The global free market as the primary force in events in developed and emerging markets had come of age. When Microsoft's CEO steps down, it is now national news, in part because this action touches so many people's lives, both within and beyond the business community. *The Apprentice* can become must-see TV, and the show's star can become president of the United States.

FRAGMENTING THE CORPORATE NARRATIVE

The advent of the Internet and the astonishing development of online technology and social media have occurred with a rapidity that appears exponential rather than evolving. For businesses navigating these dramatic changes, with app development turning into an Internet gold rush, social media platforms have become so numerous they can baffle all but the most tech savvy until the next generation of digital natives becomes the majority. At the same time, the ways both engage and fragment stakeholders have multiplied exponentially, making it even more difficult for business to control an aligned set of messages or maintain a coherent corporate narrative.

As information becomes more and more accessible, the amount of rumor, verifiably dubious behavior, and issue-based causes becomes very large. Leaving conspiracy-leaning websites aside, the information to support, say, a position against genetically modified foods is literally at anyone's fingertips who can quickly form well-organized opposition. For companies like food-processing corporation ADM, managing opposition becomes problematic, and, as later examples will suggest, ignoring opposition is perilous. Unbounded by the constraints of time or geographic location, the new social landscape is optimized for polarizing opinions, with public "likes" or "dislikes" of information sources isolating communities of thought from divergent views. With opinions hardening at the speed of thought, disrupting negative perceptions that form in real time has never been more challenging for business. Stakeholders in this new landscape not only consume information, they produce it.

In addition, the traditional journalistic rules of engagement for reporting are still evolving in social media. As the Internet eroded print journalism's revenue stream from advertising, the business of print journalism changed dramatically, with reporters now becoming social media personalities in their own right with their own brands and blogs, blurring the line between objective reporting and opinion. Whether bloggers are journalists was another debate that moderated when online news outlets such as the *Huffington Post* and *Politico*, who began as a consortium of bloggers, were awarded Pulitzer Prizes. Another casualty over the past decade has been investment in investigative journalism, making the critically acclaimed 2015 film *Spotlight* almost a nostalgic memory of a bygone era in record time. The consequence has been a diminished source of thoughtful, time-consuming investigations to act as a counterweight to the rumors and conspiracy theories that can thrive in social media. While online news sources, such as the U.S. political news fact-checking website *Politifact*, may counter sound bites, tactical corrections through such tools cannot blunt a false business narrative that can quickly gain momentum and redefine for many what is considered true.

Some early signs, however, have developed that may signal investment in investigative journalism is making a comeback. Media organizations like the New York Times, Washington Post, CNN, Fusion/Gizmodo and BuzzFeed have announced investments in investigative teams. While the catalyst for this resurgence may have been the election of Donald Trump, newly resourced investigative teams with a twenty-four-hour news cycle will have virtually unlimited news windows to report their findings on any target they deem worthy.[10]

For business—from consumer product companies to business-to-business enterprises—the consequence of passively ignoring the realities of this new landscape are substantial, particularly when, in addition to starting out at a trust deficit, public expectations for business's role in society are increasing.

On a global basis, the public is actively seeking information not only on products and brands but also monitoring the conduct and policies of companies themselves. As a consequence, in this new landscape, a corporate brand is becoming just as essential, if not more so, as product or service brands. The public is not simply actively seeking information; it is taking action on whether to purchase or boycott a product or service, as well as whether to accept or reject a position at a company or encourage someone else to do so.

Businesses that fail to factor this redefined relationship between business and society in their governance, strategies, and communications risk not only losing customers and public support for their license to operate, but also attracting and retaining their next generation of talent.

2

CLOSING THE GAP IN THE
NEW SOCIAL LANDSCAPE

In the coming years, modes of communication will change
more than they have in the previous century as businesses
adopt new ways of engaging stakeholders through social networks. Connecting effectively in this new landscape is less
about refining and pushing out the perfect corporate message. Instead, it is more about a corporation's interactive
exchanges with stakeholders and the quality and authenticity of the engagement itself.

The current pace of emerging new capabilities means
today's hot new buzz-worthy digital technology quickly
becomes yesterday's news. Today, virtual reality, initially
deployed in personal headset devices, is being used on the
New York Times website to provide users with the virtual
experience of "being" at an event, like the U.S. presidential nominating conventions. Given the appeal and credibility of firsthand observation and direct experience,
which research has shown increases trust and believability,
corporations could well integrate virtual reality into their

corporate narratives, allowing their audiences to experience their narratives via new channels as the Internet of Things continues to expand. Beyond virtual reality, IBM, in partnership with Memorial Sloan Kettering Cancer Center, is using artificial intelligence, or cognitive computing as IBM prefers to call it, in its Watson for Oncology computing system to provide clinicians with evidence-based treatment options that best align with the unique aspects of a patient's disease.

Although modes of communication are quickly evolving, we can still observe a good deal from current means. Social media tends not so much to supplant but enhance a set of concepts—corporate branding, corporate identity, reputation management, and proactive risk management—which have substantially developed over the last ten years. This chapter provides a strategic framework for those concepts to close the trust–expectations gap in the new social landscape. Having established an overall strategic framework, subsequent chapters will provide more depth and detail on the key elements of that strategic framework.

ANYONE WITH A SMARTPHONE

Today, anyone with a smartphone can change the trajectory of a business. Crises can strike at the root of corporate and industry identity marking a moment when the integrity of a corporation or an entire industry can become a trending public discussion on social media. Depending on the trigger for discussion, an exchange of information can quickly morph into a movement. This new landscape for conducting business should be top of mind for corporate C-suites and boards. Despite the enhanced threat posed by social media instantly empowering distrustful stakeholders with high expectations, however, corporate scandals continue at an unabated pace: Volkswagen's software defeating Environmental Protection Agency emissions tests; General Motors allegedly hiding internal data on defective ignition switches leading to fatalities; *League of Denial*'s exposé of the National Football League's alleged suppression of the extent of concussion and chronic traumatic encephalopathy among players,[1] and Wells Fargo's aggressive sales tactics for growth, to name but a few.

In this new context, previously reliable tools to build public support and mitigate negative issues are proving increasingly inadequate. Not so long ago, for example, corporate philanthropy was a central component of corporate risk mitigation and reputation building: companies encouraged employees to donate to charities like the United Way, and businesses' signature philanthropic programs and community relations made deposits in corporate "goodwill" banks. In fact, some of the most prestigious foundations and endowments today were begun to rehabilitate the reputation of golden-age "robber barons" with the help of foundational figures in public relations. Done well, philanthropy by itself still makes good sense as one piece of an overall business strategy. A sophisticated example can be seen in the Canon ads in *National Geographic*. Canon sponsored wildlife preservation, advertising the fact with striking photographs in *National Geographic* and, with sufficient subtlety, encouraging photography in a journal known for its excellence in photography.

Philanthropy done awkwardly, however, leaves a company open to the charge of using it as a marketing tool. The difference today is that the resulting negative visibility moves at the speed of social media. In just a matter of weeks during the 2016 U.S. presidential election campaign, for example, controversies involving the Trump Foundation morphed from a media story into fines, government investigations, and New York State enforcement cease-and-desist orders. *Washington Post* reporter David Fahrenthold won the 2017 Pulitzer Prize for his thorough investigative reporting on the Trump Foundation. What was unique, however, was the power-assist Fahrenthold got from his legion of Twitter followers in the new social landscape who helped him track down leads, effectively crowdsourcing his investigation.[2]

As with philanthropy, in a previous era, corporate television ad buys or full-page position statements in newspapers could be the centerpiece of issue management strategies. Even today, such strategies persist as part of the mix; one might go as far as to say they are elements of elaborate media rituals in which effectiveness in the new communications frontier is balanced by expectations that some traditional forms of corporate communication be used. Still, by themselves, philanthropy and corporate advertising are popguns in the new social landscape, insufficient to contain issues that can quickly threaten an organization's ability to implement strategy or even to operate.

NEW BUSINESS GUARD RAILS

Even in previous eras, corporate advertising had its limits. Union Carbide once ran advertisements stating that it was bringing prosperity to India. Then came the 1984 Bhopal disaster: a toxic chemical release that initially killed more than two thousand people, with more to follow. No mitigation is possible for a corporate accident of that scale. BP's "Beyond Petroleum" campaign followed the traditional corporate playbook of brand building through a corporate advertising campaign that attempted to make the case for its investment in alternative energy, only to be eviscerated by the Deepwater Horizon oil spill in 2010.

In both examples, however, the failed effectiveness of the corporate advertisements was not simply a matter of bad timing. The horrific disasters would have obliterated any corporate campaign. But the disasters themselves were also not a function of bad luck caused by forces external to the companies, such as the case with the Tylenol product tampering crisis that resulted in poisoning deaths in 1982. With both Bhopal and Deepwater, the tragedies were rooted in corporate strategies and operational decisions at the heart of each company's business model.

Union Carbide had opted to run the Bhopal pesticide plant through a 51 percent–owned subsidiary, using methyl isocyanate gas as an intermediate in its manufacturing process to produce Sevin, their branded pesticide, in contrast to a methyl isocyanate–free process used by some other manufacturers. As demand for pesticides decreased in the early 1980s, Union Carbide's excess production of the potentially lethal methyl isocyanate required on-site storage. Water leaking into an MIC storage tank triggered a runaway chemical reaction causing the tragedy.[3] Whether the leak was caused by sabotage, as Union Carbide maintained, or inadequate maintenance, as critics have claimed, the trigger for the tragedy was inherent in Union Carbide's business decision to manufacture Sevin using methyl isocyanate without sufficiently managing the risk in that decision, whether through appropriate maintenance or more extensive operational oversight of its subsidiary.

In the case of Deepwater Horizon, it was the offshore drilling contractor Transocean, not BP, that operated the ill-fated rig, drilling at a depth of 5,000 feet to create an oil well 18,360 feet deep, using advanced systems to address the complexity of the drilling operations from suppliers like Halliburton. Following the disaster, BP's attempt to divert blame to Transocean and Halliburton ended with the court declaring BP guilty of gross negligence and willful misconduct, apportioning 67 percent of the blame to BP, 30 percent to Transocean, and 3 percent to Halliburton.[4] While many complex factors contributed to the blowout that killed 11 of the 126 people on board when the rig exploded, the technology that had enabled deep-water drilling had clearly exceeded the technology needed to reliably address the risks inherent in drilling at that depth, or to remedy a failure at 5,000 feet below sea level, as the real-time images of 53,000 barrels of oil per day gushing from the wellhead for over three months demonstrated. The use of that drilling technology without sufficient contingency remedies was BP's business decision, and it was inherent in their business model.

Previously, a combination of government regulation and litigation or the threat of litigation operated as preemptive guard rails to restrain risky business decisions that might lead to class actions or massive personal injury disasters like those seen with Bhopal and Deepwater. With government gridlock setting new standards for inaction without consequence and the rollback of business regulations, the effectiveness of those guard rails has waned. Instead, the new social landscape in which businesses now operate is becoming a forceful check, demonstrating its power to address intractable, long-standing issues with urgency.

RULES OF ENGAGEMENT 2.0

Mylan's EpiPen pricing controversy provides a compelling example of the changing rules of engagement in the relationship between business and society. A leading global generic and specialty pharmaceutical company, Mylan acquired the EpiPen, an epinephrine autoinjector, from Merck in 2007. A branded product, the EpiPen is the most widely available device for reversing potentially fatal allergic reactions. Those at risk typically must purchase many pens to keep at various locations, including the home, school, and workplace.

Like many pharmaceutical companies trying to mitigate the negative impact of the long-standing societal concern over ever-increasing drug prices, Mylan had established patient assistance programs to offset out-of-pocket costs for the EpiPen, reportedly spending more than $10 million since 2011 in educational sponsorships and grants. It had also engaged with prominent third-party groups, including Food and Allergy Research and Education, the Asthma and Allergy Foundation of America, and the Allergy and Asthma Network, to advance its patient education.[5]

While most pharmaceutical companies use this kind of stakeholder outreach and engagement to mitigate the risk of eroding public support owing to the high price of drugs in the United States, Mylan found those tactics completely inadequate to address the tsunami of social media outrage that developed in just a matter of weeks. In the summer of 2016, as parents were restocking EpiPens for the back-to-school season, they suddenly faced a cost of $600 for a pair of EpiPens, rather than the $100 they had previously been paying before Mylan began raising the price by a cumulative 500 percent.

The architecture of this quickly developing outrage provides a compelling example of the web-enabled activist environment in which business now operates. Today, a global community of engaged information-seekers can quickly form communities of thought ready to act when their expectations of the role of business in society are not met. In July 2016, a web-savvy New Yorker, Mellini Kantayya, converted her ongoing Facebook conversation with friends about EpiPen pricing into an online petition to stop the EpiPen price gouging. The petition was targeted at lawmakers and administered through the website Petition2Congress.com. In just 45 days, the petition garnered more than 80,000 signatures and generated more than 121,000 letters to Congress. Parent activists from websites like PeanutAllergyMom.com and AllergyKids.com escalated what had begun as an individual protest into a nationwide movement. From a standing start, the issue was suddenly covered by all major media outlets, and Mylan's CEO, Heather Bresch, was facing inquiries from the United States Senate Committee on the Judiciary and testifying before the United States House of Representatives.[6]

By mid-October 2016, Mylan's original effort to stem social outrage by offering patients coupons had evolved into offering a generic version of the branded EpiPen at a much reduced price, and Mylan quickly settled a dispute with the United States Department of Justice, agreeing to pay $465 million to resolve rebate liability claims. The government maintained that Mylan had classified the EpiPen as a generic drug under the Medicaid social health care program while at the same time marketing the device as a branded product. Mylan's inappropriate classification of the EpiPen as generic dramatically reduced the rebate the company owed the government under the program, inflating the product's profit margin as the company increased its pricing, making the EpiPen a major factor in the company's overall drug sales. Even after the settlement, Mylan continued to face inquiries from the U.S. Securities and Exchange Commission and U.S. Senate investigations.[7]

"IT JUST FELT NEFARIOUS"

Ironically, Mylan's generic drug business could have put the company in the position of being part of the solution to the growing social concerns over drug pricing and access. Instead, Mylan marketed the EpiPen as a branded product to severe allergy sufferers having few alternative options and aggressively spiked its price at multiple increments while expanding its profit margin by misclassifying it as generic under Medicaid. Mylan displayed a shocking lack of insight and concern for the stakeholder impact of its business strategies. The more Mylan's profits grew because of its EpiPen business strategies, the more it multiplied its negative stakeholder impact, stoking outrage even more. In an interview with the *New York Times*, Bresch articulated her business philosophy for the company: "I am running a business. I am a for-profit business. I am not hiding from that."[8] Bresch's statement harkens back to how business was done in the earlier era discussed in chapter 1, where shareholder return was accepted as the exclusive mandate for a business. But declaring profitability as the exclusive mandate for business in today's new social landscape did not increase shareholder value, as Mylan saw its stock plunge 25 percent.

During the EpiPen controversy, Mylan's business strategy received an unfortunate third-party endorsement from Turing Pharmaceuticals' former CEO, Martin Shkreli, routinely called "the most hated man in America" in the media after raising the price of Daraprim, a drug used to treat parasitic diseases for which there was no generic alternative, from $13.50 to $750 per tablet, more than a 5,000 percent increase.[9] A Google search of "Shkreli smirk" demonstrates the seemingly permanent social media indictment of both the man and his business strategies.

In both the Mylan and Turing controversies, the CEOs attempted to shift blame for the social outrage over their drug pricing strategies to insurance companies whose high deductibles had increased patients' out-of-pocket costs. In that context, both CEOs no doubt believed their strategies to offset patient costs through coupons and patient assistance programs would sufficiently shield them from criticism. Those business strategies, however, totally missed the point of the outrage—and the new rules of engagement for doing business in the new social landscape. While exorbitant pricing may have triggered people's outrage, the motivating energy behind the widespread web-based campaign against the EpiPen price gouging was that Mylan's business strategies were just the wrong thing to do. Its strategies impacted not only patients but society as a whole:

> "It just felt nefarious," said Ms. Kantayya, whose health insurance covers the cost of EpiPens for her husband, who has an allergic condition. "Just because we are not paying for it, we are still paying for it in terms of the social cost," she said. Then she thought, "Why don't I do a petition, and maybe something can be done about this."[10]

Without a fatal disaster, as in the cases of Union Carbide and BP, and without litigation-driven media visibility or new regulations acting as a check on business excess, public expectations on what constitutes appropriate business behavior, empowered through social media, forced Mylan to change its business strategies—at least for one product.

THE PROOFS OF CHOICE: ACTIONS TAKEN AND PERSONAL EXPERIENCE

Today, the landscape for successfully managing business has fundamentally changed. Closing the trust–expectations gap for business in this new environment requires integrating stakeholder impact into corporate strategies, governance, policies, and operations with stakeholders judging with the result through the corporate decisions made and actions taken. As Corey duBrowa, former senior vice-president of global communications and international public affairs for Starbucks has observed, "The most potent contributor to trust is the commitment to taking meaningful action."[11] The new social landscape has ushered in a degree of transparency never before seen. The result: Trust must be earned through action not simply messaging.

As the EpiPen example illustrates, social media has created an ever-present, web-enabled, watchdog public, replacing Galbraith's earlier system of checks and balances on business based on regulations and unions. Actions taken, not simply promises made, are the proof of choice on the web, with a new era of citizen journalists emerging, posting visual evidence online for the public to judge for themselves. With the near-global rejection of all things "establishment," acceptance of the previous era's authorities has been replaced by the direct experience of seeing it for yourself or discovering it yourself on the web through your chosen communities of thought. The primary factor driving the public's opinions of business today is personal experience and direct engagement.[12]

Today, when online purchasing is eclipsing face-to-face business transactions, trust is table stakes for doing business and is manifested in ways not limited to one's last transaction. In everyday terms, we can see how trust has become so basic a foundation for doing business and advancing corporate strategy. If you arrange with a friend to meet at a coffee shop at an agreed time, you trust your friend to be there at the set time. If your friend is a bit early, it is reassuring to discover that the coffee shop you picked is not the one with the same name across town. If your friend is always 15 minutes late, you can factor this in with some level of annoyance or acceptance as the case may be. If the appointment is missed two or three times, or your friend turns up unreasonably late, trust erodes—trust based on personal experience.

Recognizing the power of personal experience, AT&T, which has made reliability a cornerstone of its identity, has designed their New Jersey visitors' center to demonstrate its promise of reliability in action through their visitors' direct observations. Following a standard-issue corporate video, the screen is raised to reveal a large space resembling the set of a James Bond movie. One large wall is covered with an electronic map tracking in real time every one of the millions of calls being made in the United States. Beneath the screen sit a score of employees at computer terminals. The tour guide announces to the visitors witnessing this scene that one call goes astray every two days. If you think about this, you might begin to believe that the frequency with which you get a wrong number likely has more to do with your own misdialing than phone company errors. Reliability at this level can seem almost uncanny.

If not an in-person experience engaged through a visitor center, social media platforms like Facebook provide substitutes for the private in-person connection between individuals that provides the best forum for gaining trust, providing a new kind of virtual public space where opinion might be formed. These virtual "meeting places" are what the communication scholar Jürgen Habermas calls the "public sphere," the all-important space where, for example, the eighteenth-century coffee houses shaped what people should think as they sat and read a then-new phenomenon, the newspaper, such as *The Spectator* or *The Rambler*. Addison and Steel's *Spectator*, deliberately sought to frame the coffee house discussions to focus on codes of behavior for an emerging middle class as tradesmen became gentlemen of substance. Not coincidentally, coffee houses were also the original sites of the London stock exchange.

STAKEHOLDER IMPACT AND THE BUSINESS MODEL

Closing the trust–expectations gap for business in the new social landscape requires integrating stakeholder impact into corporate strategies, governance, policies, and operations. The starting point must be understanding the impact of a business through the lens of the stakeholder, not through the corporate lens, something Mylan's pricing strategy failed to do. Many strategic stakeholder models illustrate business management as the hub of a wheel surrounded by the spokes representing stakeholders, including investors, suppliers, employees, and the community.

Not long ago, marketers rediscovered the centrality of the customer. The next turn of the wheel has been for management theory to consider employees as central to the identity of an organization, to conceive of corporate identity as beginning with the actual organization, made up of managers and the people they manage. As the University of Virginia Darden Graduate School of Business professor Edward Hess has shown, companies with the highest bottom-line growth are also those where all employees are aligned with the idea of the business, including understanding the company's business strategy.[13]

The wheel model, however, understates the fluid, fungible reality of stakeholders. One contemporary, commonsense attribute of stakeholder theory is that categories are not exclusive. Employees, for example, are also customers and may have strong affinities with environmental or social causes that involve their workplace or even the products or services their companies produce or provide. More importantly, the wheel model implies a static relationship. But, as the Mylan example vividly demonstrates, stakeholders wear many hats—those of customers, parents, activists, bloggers, and even shareholders—and are dynamically engaged, with their potential impact on a business empowered at an unprecedented level through social media.

In fact, the Champion Brand research suggests a new category—stake*brokers*—to distinguish a new category of influential stakeholders in the new social landscape whose empowered, collective activism is resetting the relationship between business and society. Rather than the more familiar key opinion leaders, who are often determined by the depth of their knowledge on a particular subject, stakebrokers are distinguished by the breadth and diversity of their engagement, making them pivotal players in today's critically important stakeholder mapping of the social landscape of an issue or a corporate or product brand.

The EpiPen outrage is a case study of this new category of stakebrokers and their impact. With 165,000 followers on Facebook and Twitter, Robyn O'Brien, the founder of AllergyKids.com, along with some other stakebrokers, was pivotal in the rapid escalation of the issue. Following Mellini Kantayya's creation of the "Stop the EpiPen Price Gouging" petition on Petition2Congress.com on July 11, 2016, O'Brien wrote a Facebook post on the EpiPen issue on July 21, 2016, which was shared 727 times. Her second post on the issue was shared 477 times, after which she was joined by another parent activist, Becky Bergman, in urging followers to sign Kantayya's petition. O'Brien then coined the Twitter hashtag #EpiGate, triggering a mushrooming of mainstream media interest, and her additional plea to sign the petition was shared 972 times. The term "multiplier effect" does not seem adequate here. Perhaps a spiral should replace the wheel in the strategic stakeholder business model.

Stakebrokers working through social media can instantaneously create a thick, active media environment where transparency may well arrive far more quickly than businesses are prepared for, as Mylan certainly found. In an unusual correspondence of cause and effect, however, social media may well offer a promising channel to bridge the gap between eroding trust and increasing expectations, even while the volume of available undifferentiated information can widen it. The once prominent glossy annual report, for example, pales in comparison to a well-managed corporate website as a tool for explaining the modern corporation. And social media provides unprecedented potential for stakeholder engagement. In the case of Mylan, the dynamic influence of stakebrokers in escalating the EpiPen outrage could have been tracked by the company had they been monitoring this new category of influencers rather than the more familiar list of key opinion leaders monitored by many corporations. Once detected, and before the outrage reached critical scale, Mylan could have taken more effective corrective actions and given credit for those actions to the insight gained from these stakebrokers.

In the hyper-connected world in which business is now conducted, corporations that have integrated the outside-in stakeholder view of their business strategies, policies, governance, and operations have recognized that their critics now have nearly limitless communication platforms. Engaged companies have "listening" rooms monitoring social media traffic. Informed employees take part in chat rooms, self-identifying but setting the record straight concerning incorrect information and promising action on flaws. Critics' concerns, now accessible to all on the web and via social media, can act as significant early warning signals of problematic issues or provide information about when a known issue is reaching new levels of concern. Labeling corporate critics as anti-business "activists" should be a red flag of thinking that is no longer useful. Moreover, working directly with responsible critics builds trust as much as the tried-and-true technique of using third-party experts to make a point or change opinion.

STAKEHOLDER BLIND SPOTS

Even the most committed corporation, however, can fail to anticipate the stakeholder impact of their business strategies, complicating efforts to close the trust–expectations gap. Getting out of the business bubble and stepping away from corporate culture to understand the sometimes-unintended consequences of a business strategy or policy often requires a concerted effort to see a business's actions through a stakeholder lens, to anticipate an issue "through the windshield" rather than "through the rearview mirror" following a crisis.

Every company and every industry faces one or more issues directly connected to its business model that places it at risk of reputation damage, as well as a financial loss, an eroded market share, or, when unattended, a crisis. From insurance, we borrow the concept of "inherent vice" and modify it to the notion of an "inherent negative," a business model's latent negative stakeholder impacts that increase as the company grows, explored in detail in chapter 3. If an inherent negative is left unidentified or unaddressed, the more successful a business is, the greater the negative impacts will be, multiplying the enterprise's risks, ranging from financial and reputation losses to the erosion of its fundamental license to operate.

Mylan's business strategy of escalating the price of the EpiPen as a branded product while at the same time building wider profit margins by misclassifying it as generic to reduce its Medicaid rebates is a classic example. As these strategies increased Mylan's revenue and profit growth, they also increased the number of stakeholders negatively impacted who had few alternatives to this potentially life-saving product. Growing and profiting from a negative stakeholder impact, no matter whether the impact is unrealized or unintended, makes inherent negatives a powerful accelerant for public outrage. In fact, today, the sphere of inherent negatives that affect business has expanded to include larger social problems. These pressing social issues—including obesity, privacy, carbon footprint, open sourcing, and fair labor practices—hang over the heads of many businesses and industries like the Sword of Damocles.

Many corporations have begun to examine and remedy the negative stakeholder impact integrated into their product or service supply chain or life cycle. However, sources of inherent negatives, as in the case of Mylan, can also be a function of corporate policy and governance. The important point here is that in today's instantly transparent social landscape, once an inherent negative has gained public traction, it widens the gap between the public's trust in business and their expectations for business conduct. When that happens, investing in building brand and reputation becomes, at best, an ineffective distraction until action is taken to mitigate the negative stakeholder impact.

The Deepwater Horizon disaster is again instructive. The disaster revealed the risks inherent in the company's business model—accessing oil though offshore drilling in deep water without effective interventions when things went wrong. Despite using joint ventures to conduct its drilling, BP's inherent negative extended through the supply chain. Years after the rig exploded, BP continues to make reparations and settle litigation. The leading factor in rebuilding its reputation will not be corporate advertising. Instead, it will come from the extensive constructive actions BP has taken in the affected region to mitigate damage through direct community engagement, allowing citizens to personally experience interactions with BP. Once BP has reached a breakeven point with the stakeholders it has directly impacted, it will be in a position to more broadly rebuild its reputation.

The key point here is the codependent relationship between mitigating the risk posed by inherent negatives and building upside brand and reputation. CVS Pharmacy recognized this codependency when they jettisoned tobacco sales, a product with clear inherent negatives, as a threshold action prior to initiating a strategic business pivot of its identity from a generic, large-chain drug store to a health care provider and supplier. The resulting dramatic $2 billion loss in tobacco sales captured media attention in a way that allowed a company not necessarily known for close bonds with consumers to differentiate its brand in a compelling way. Companies that manage risks from inherent negatives in this way are managing proactively, anticipating and addressing their businesses' inherent risks in the new social landscape as key deliverables for corporate strategic planning. Their business strategies address both sides of the equation: mitigating risks while simultaneously advancing their brands in a way that meets the rising bar of stakeholder expectations.

As a postscript, CVS has also begun selling a generic version of the EpiPen for roughly one-third the initial list price of Mylan's generic version.[14]

CLOSING THE TRUST-EXPECTATIONS GAP

Recognizing the need to advance brands by closing the trust–expectations gap for business, many different business theories and models have emerged, among them shared value, corporate authenticity, corporate social responsibility, and triple-bottom-line reporting. Each contributes to an evolution of how businesses can better align with societal expectations while also creating financial value. However, the value of these theories and models diminishes if they are used in isolation or, worse yet, as competing strategies.

To address the need for a more comprehensive and integrated framework for managing the changing relationship between society and business, the Champion Brand model brings together different theories on the relationship between business and society, including traditional ways of examining corporate reputation, brand marketing, early work from the Arthur W. Page Society on authenticity and corporate character,[15] and the concepts of shared advocacy and shared value. Together, these perspectives build a comprehensive model for understanding brand effectiveness in the twenty-first century, where corporations no longer have full control over their messages or reputations given the power shift to external, web-enabled stakeholders. This model offers a framework for integrating stakeholder expectations into a company's business model—its business strategies, governance, and policies—to mitigate risk and build brand.

The Champion Brand model has at the base of its "pyramid" a foundation of "alignment"; that is, the alignment of corporate behavior with stakeholder expectations—and communication with internal and external audiences. Once an aspiration, alignment is now considered a minimum requirement to meet society's rising expectations. It is a starting point of departure. Meeting or exceeding customer expectations has been the bedrock of total quality management since the seeds of quality management first emerged in the 1920s, including ISO 9000, a set of international standards on quality management and quality assurance, and quality award programs like the Deming Prize for total quality management and the Malcolm Baldrige National Quality Award.

What has changed in the new social landscape is the detailed, around-the-clock global examination of *how* a company aligns its strategies and operations to meet not only customer expectations but also multiple stakeholder and stakebroker expectations, from its choice and treatment of suppliers to the stakeholder impact of its supply chain management. Starbucks' fair-trade decision regarding its sourcing policies for coffee, for example, was a response to criticism from nongovernmental organizations—organizations that rate far more positively on trust measurements than corporations. Fair-trade coffee does not make up the bulk of Starbucks' coffee supply. Instead, the company targets "ethically sourced" coffee, with 99 percent of its coffee certified by either Coffee and Farmer Equity Practices (CAFE) or Fairtrade.[16] Regardless, the company's brand proposition was such that the company could not ignore questions about how it was sourcing its coffee.

Aligning corporate behavior with stakeholder expectations has become more fully integrated into business operations through advances in corporate social responsibility as companies audit their supply chains and analyze their products' lifecycle impact on multiple stakeholders, engaging stakeholders and third parties to better understand an issue from multiple points of view. Reporting on stakeholder impact is also evolving, as an increasing number of companies have adopted triple-bottom-line reporting that accounts for social and environmental performance, as well as financial performance.[17] Even with these advances to close the trust–expectations gap, skeptics would argue that not all adopters of triple-bottom-line reporting include people and planet in their core values; in such cases, reporting becomes a perfunctory exercise.

AUTHENTICITY THAT WITHSTANDS TRANSPARENCY

Beyond the minimum requirement of alignment, the next level of Champion Brand's model is the "authenticity" of business objectives consistent with values and vision, an authenticity that can withstand transparency. In a sense, these are at once admirable goals but also requirements for managing risk. An authentic company or brand is hard to imagine without a viable and vibrant corporate identity. In this context, corporate identity is a more strategic and more comprehensive approach than a consistently displayed logo or a well-implemented set of visual identity guidelines. Just ask Ikea, whose look and feel have been copied in China by 11 Furniture, including its blue-and-yellow color scheme, mock-up rooms, and cafeteria-style restaurant, with no connection to Ikea itself.[18] An authentic corporate identity should be something that is understood internally and compelling externally. The corporate brands that make a difference are simply those that are comprehensible expressions of an organization's values, whether it is astonishing customer service at a company like Zappos or the earnest desire to find a medical solution at a biotech startup.

As many corporations are realizing, employees are at the strategic center of an authentic corporation, creating greater interest in a more strategic approach to employee engagement. The days of employee communication as simply rooted in an internal magazine are long gone. Because employees are also customers, they may have strong affinities with environmental or social causes that involve their workplace and are affected by public and media perceptions of their organization.

Nicholas Ind maintains that brands are defined by people. Including employees as a core constituent of corporate identity can convert the concept of employees as cost into cultures with competitive advantage. People trust someone they feel is authentic, someone who is "being himself or herself."

At some point, authentic organizations gain greater levels of trust and put meaning back into phrases like "Our people come first." Internal social media platforms within a company enable communities of shared interest and knowledge to flourish. Blogs and tweets, even with clear policies about their use, make corporate culture transparent. As will be discussed in chapter 4, coming to terms with a company's character and finding authentic ways to express that character are where things start.

YOU CHANGE IT. IT CHANGES YOU.

Closely related to authenticity is the next level of the Champion Brand model: "attachment." Emotional attachment has long been recognized as essential to building a product brand or even a corporate brand. What has changed in the new social landscape is the importance of an emotional attachment to the company itself. Certainly, a description of a brand starts with its attributes. But when these attributes mean something more, that has a good deal to do with emotion. As a manager at Nissan once remarked, there is no logical argument for purchasing an Infiniti FX. Yet when Nissan evolved from a brand that sold cars at a discount to a brand competing on the level of Toyota and Honda, it gained attributes such as a more differentiated design, a bit more power, and greater investment in interiors. It managed to jump to another level with the brilliant "Shift" advertising campaign and the company's commitment to renewing its brand, which the new CEO, Carlos Ghosn, claimed added $2,000 to the value of each car.[19]

Expanding on the concept of attachment, brands now seek to relate to customers in different ways, changing them as they change products. A clever manifestation of this is an Internet advertisement for Nike that shows a young woman exercising, walking and running throughout the day, a young man engaged in bouts of competitive sports, and a young slacker lounging on his couch. As each activity is shown, those viewing the ad award M&Ms to those of whom they approve, with the couch potato getting no reward. In the final seconds, the fellow on the couch grabs a skateboard and performs feats so extraordinary that he wins the most M&Ms.

Nike, both the company and the brand, can appeal to a tech-savvy demographic because years before it had successfully addressed an inherent negative in its business model of sourcing its branded clothing through contract manufacturers having substandard labor conditions, which led to a campus-inspired boycott. Nike's extensive constructive actions included what are now considered role-model codes of conduct for its contract manufacturing suppliers with strictly enforced compliance. Nike successfully mitigated the risk posed by inherent negatives in its business model, enabling its brand to survive the controversy and the company to resume its growth trajectory.

The Apple brand, both the company and its products, present the most obvious example of the power of attachment. Apple sells things: cool things, beautifully designed (as has been said, the iPod was the next thing Sony could have made after the Walkman). Its devices are highly customizable so that no one really has the same thing—they can't have your iPhone (or your Twitter followers). The Apple ecosystem contains the owner's identity in a two-way engagement—you change it, it changes you. Apple's brand promise has incorporated the essential risk-mitigating promise of privacy, a promise Apple fiercely defended with its refusal to comply with the FBI's request to unlock an iPhone belonging to Syed Rizwan Farook, who, along with Tashfeen Malik, killed 14 people in San Bernardino, California, on December 2, 2015.

Attachment to new technology firms like Apple can be so strong that it is taken for granted as a force of progress (with progress seen as very much an Enlightenment ideal), demonstrating a strong countervailing vector to low trust in business. As testimony to the strength of such attachment, technology firms like Apple are seemingly given a "hall pass" from social outrage if their products, for example, are made in substandard factories in China and do not meet the expectations normally applied to a business. Indeed, it would be fair to say that Americans in particular have a sometimes paradoxical "love–hate" relationship with corporations they "love to hate." While not consistently expected to "do the right thing," companies such as Apple, Facebook, Google, and Twitter, which account for large amounts of the Dow Jones valuation, are, at the same time, expected to solve our problems, not the least of which is leading the economy out of recession.

ADVANCING TO SHARED ADVOCACY

"Advocacy" sits at the peak of the Champion Brand model, recognizing the potential for companies to become advocates or "champions" for interests that benefit their businesses and also benefit their stakeholders and society. Companies that meet expectations for alignment, authenticity, and attachment and then advance to this level become so-called Champion Brands—whether a consumer brand or a business-to-business company. Champion Brands achieve demonstrably better results, including improved sales and customer loyalty, greater employee retention and engagement, and a more favorable regulatory environment. As a result, they are better positioned to weather crises and ultimately deliver greater shareholder value than brands that have not met the requirements of the four tiers of the Champion Brand model.[20]

In fact, an analysis of the relationship between the Champion Brand Index and market capitalization shows at a 99 percent confidence level, that for every one-point increase in a company's score on the Champion Brand Index, a company's market capitalization on average increases by $1.5 billion. That means that when all other financial factors are treated equally, being a Champion Brand gives a company a $1.5 billon premium.[21]

Companies that both proactively mitigate their business model's inherent negatives and advance their brands by finding platforms for shared advocacy benefitting both their business and society are building trust and meeting rising expectations in the new social landscape. Patagonia provides a clear example of this strategy in action with its "Reason for Being" statement, which addresses both sides of the equation: mitigating the risk posed by inherent negatives in its business model while building a Champion Brand:

OUR REASON FOR BEING

Patagonia grew out of a small company that made tools for climbers. Alpinism remains at the heart of a worldwide business that still makes clothes for climbing—as well as for skiing, snowboarding, surfing, fly fishing, paddling and trail running. These are all silent sports. None require a motor; none deliver the cheers of a crowd. In each sport, reward comes in the form of hard-won grace and moments of connection between us and nature.

Our values reflect those of a business started by a band of climbers and surfers, and the minimalist style they promoted. The approach we take towards product design demonstrates a bias for simplicity and utility.

For us at Patagonia, a love of wild and beautiful places demands participation in the fight to save them, and to help reverse the steep decline in the overall environmental health of our planet. We donate our time, services and at least 1 percent of our sales to hundreds of grassroots environmental groups all over the world who work to help reverse the tide.

We know that our business activity—from lighting stores to dyeing shirts—creates pollution as a by-product. So we work steadily to reduce those harms. We use recycled polyester in many of our clothes and only organic, rather than pesticide-intensive, cotton.

Staying true to our core values during thirty-plus years in business has helped us create a company we're proud to run and work for. And our focus on making the best products possible has brought us success in the marketplace.[22]

Extending the Patagonia example, the need to work both sides of the equation (mitigating risks from inherent negatives and building brand) can apply to an entire industry. The apparel industry's offshore sourcing of low-cost labor has conditioned an entire generation to expect clothing so inexpensive that a previous era's required junior high school class for girls learning how to sew ("home economics" classes) is now a memory shared primarily by grandmothers.

Although Nike led the way for the apparel industry to mitigate inherent negatives from the labor practices of its off-shore suppliers, the industry's low-cost business model has other inherent negatives to address. Clothing is now a disposable commodity, with the majority winding up in landfills. The United States Environmental Protection Agency estimates that Americans alone dispose of about 12.8 million tons of clothing annually, with the average American throwing away 70 pounds of clothing and other textiles each year. While approximately 15 percent of post-use textiles are donated, 85 percent goes into landfills. The more the industry grows, the more waste its business model produces, a classic inherent negative.[23]

Beyond efforts at clothing recycling and reuse, the apparel industry is now exploring new systems designed to enable generating fiber for new products from recovered apparel, substantially reducing waste and also consuming less of a dwindling water supply to grow cotton. This is a work in process with the impetus coming from growing pressure on companies and the industry as a whole from web-enabled communities to address a societal need.[24]

Like Patagonia, UPS provides another example of a company applying a comprehensive framework for integrating socially responsible behavior into its business model, both mitigating its inherent risks while advancing its brand, from its supply chain management through its employee policies and product portfolios. Central to UPS's business model is a single network that integrates all its modes of pickup and delivery, giving it greater logistical flexibility in selecting the most efficient and least carbon-intensive mode of delivery. Given UPS's core business of delivery, its carbon footprint, if left unmitigated, would be a classic example of an inherent negative. The more its delivery business grows, the greater its carbon footprint.[25]

Behind UPS's performance is a deep commitment to technological and logistical infrastructure, expressed in their "We love logistics" advertising campaign which is as resonant with the complexity of today's delivery challenges as it is with UPS's heritage. Founder Jim Casey established the principle of finding shorter and faster delivery routes on his bicycle in Seattle. Beyond logistics, UPS has the strongest track record in the United States of promoting employees from "line" positions within the company, such as drivers and delivery center supervisors, to management positions, including its current CEO, David Abney.

The lesson of UPS is the extent to which its use of technology and its socially responsible behavior are baked into its business model: Efficient delivery saves money and reduces the company's carbon footprint; its focus on logistics and its technological infrastructure is a function of an engineering culture and its heritage; employees' engagement with the company and the company's commitment to its employees make UPS trustworthy for consumers on a daily basis and a responsible corporate citizen for many stakeholders. UPS's actions have credibility and authenticity because they are closely aligned with its business model and corporate philosophy.

As we will see in the following chapters, closing the gap between the public's trust in and expectations for business in the hyper-engaged twenty-first century will be achieved a brick at a time. Companies must first understand and then mitigate the risks inherent in their businesses, assessing them through the lens of those impacted and then building their identity, brand values, and reputation through strategies and actions that advance both their interests and those of their stakeholders, particularly as an engaged and activated public converts unresolved issues into urgent matters. Getting ahead of society's expectations curve can open new fields for competitive advantage. In this way, new and believable stories will—along with trust—regain meaning.

A recent trip to the New York International Auto Show is instructive. As might be expected, Volvos were displayed under the banner of safety. Nissan, a resurgent brand, displayed its new brand message of "Shift." Toyota, with a first-mover advantage in hybrids, emphasized quality and innovation.

Toyota famously built its reputation for quality, and its remarkable market share, through its trust in employees. If a defect was found on the assembly line, a worker pulled a cord, the line was stopped, and the problem was fixed. Toyota's reputation for quality over time became so strong that the corporate crisis involving gas pedals accelerating by themselves cut into the corporation's core identity. After the dust settled, the crisis turned out to have had more to do with bungling the response to the crisis than either a defect causing the gas pedals to stick or a potential electronic issue. Directly following the crisis, Toyota lost its long-coveted place as holder of the largest market share in North America. As conventional wisdom has it, it is not the scandal, it's the cover-up—or in this case, the perception of one. The unfortunate twist here is that Toyota was vindicated, with the bungled response to the crisis being the true crisis. Still, through a reputation built on its continually reliable products, the company can regain consumer confidence after an inept response. Today, reflecting the increased emphasis on businesses' social impact, Toyota promotes quality and innovation and also the notion of "enriching lives," connecting its production of hybrid cars to improving the environment.

Two anecdotes may be taken as emblematic as we close this chapter. On a bicycle fan chat room, a participant posted about how to unlock an expensive Kryptonite bicycle lock with a Bic pen. This led to Kryptonite re-engineering the lock from a tubular to a disc design, communicating that the problem was solved, and offering a free exchange for locks using the tubular design. The second anecdote involves a young man checking into a hotel of a well-known chain and tweeting his disappointment with his room to a friend. Soon after, the front desk called the young man and offered him a room upgrade. This response resulted in a tweet from the man praising the hotel. The case of the bicycle lock highlights the heightened level of risk posed by the web. The hotel incident demonstrates how social media presents an opportunity for businesses to build positive relationships with their customers.

3

INHERENT NEGATIVES:
MANAGING RISK AND REPUTATION

In *Against the Gods: The Remarkable Story of Risk*, Peter Bernstein persuasively argues that business took its modern form, and could only take its modern form, once it became possible to adequately assess risk through the concept of probability, developed in seventeenth-century France. Probability provided the ability to make predictions based on statistical analysis, which "lies at the core of our modern market economy" and continues to dominate managerial thinking and management education today.[1] A reliance on the predictive power of statistics has had numerous consequences. By the late nineteenth century, insurance companies could accumulate enough data, for example, that they could predict one's longevity with an accuracy that many of us would find best left to actuarial tables in the way people now decide whether to discover if their DNA has an unwelcome kink. The insurance industry also has a theory called inherent vice, not in the sense of continuing to smoke but in the inherent vice, for example, of insuring a ship that might hit a reef and sink.

This book suggests that the importance of understanding business risk in the twenty-first century has taken on new meaning given the context of declining trust and increasing expectations, as well as a new urgency for action in the era of a global, empowered watchdog public working around the clock. As briefly introduced in the discussion of Mylan's EpiPen controversy in chapter 2, we have applied the insurance concept of inherent vice to the notion of an "inherent negative" which this chapter details in the context of the new social landscape.

A BUSINESS RISK WAKEUP CALL

The strategic surprise of the 2007–2009 global financial crisis provided a wakeup call for C-suite management and their boards of directors to re-examine their predictive risk management protocols, with a particular interest in strategic risk management. Ram Charan's *Owning Up: The 14 Questions Every Board Member Needs to Ask*, published in 2009, quickly made the must-read short list for corporate board members. "Risk," wrote globally recognized business consultant Charan, "is an integral part of every company's strategy; when boards review strategy, they have to be forceful in asking the CEO what risks are inherent in the strategy."[2]

Often, business risk assessment has been confined to a data-driven analyses based on technically oriented financial or engineering assessment protocols. However, particularly in the new social landscape with empowered stakeholders on social media, that technical bias can overlook the very real potential business risks from fast-moving issues gaining traction and substantially disrupting business strategies.

Shell, a world leader in oil and gas exploration and production whose Brent Spar encounter with Greenpeace began this book, has clearly recognized the blind spot a technical bias in risk assessment can foster. Operating in some of the most challenging geographies in the world, Shell acknowledges that its industry has made substantial progress in addressing its technical challenges, but not in its capacity to manage nontechnical challenges, which arise from its interactions with its broad range of stakeholders:

> Non-technical risks are the most common cause of project delays and most likely to be underestimated and overlooked but have the potential to cause significant erosions of project value when they manifest at project level and in extreme cases significant portfolio value erosion, when they manifest at corporate or industry level.

Shell has proactively integrated assessing nontechnical risks (which they call NTRs) into their way of doing business. NTRs are part of Shell's impact assessment process to ascertain stakeholder interests and concerns at the project concept stage when the project viability is being evaluated. According to Shell, well-managed NTRs have upside impact on a project's financial and operational success and have the potential to positively differentiate the company.[3]

EMBEDDED STAKEHOLDER IMPACT

Any business has a dominant risk or set of risks that are inherent to the business model itself. Thus, the more successful a company is, the more potential harm an unrecognized risk can cause, substantially magnifying the company's risk profile.

Inherent negatives are business risks derived from the negative stakeholder impact of latent attributes in a given business model; for example, attributes in the product or service itself, impacts from the upstream product or service lifecycle supply chain from sourcing raw materials or service capabilities to the downstream use and disposal of the product or service by customers, and impacts from C-suite governance and policies as management stewards the business model. Because inherent negatives are embedded in a company's strategies, operations, or policies, as the company grows, its unmitigated negative stakeholder impacts also grow. When an enterprise's growth and success also multiply its negative impacts, outrage can follow and with it, the potential for boycotts, constraints on the license to operate, and disrupted implementation of strategic plans.

The growing sophistication of global supply chain management and the adoption of corporate social responsibility initiatives have allowed many companies to discover and proactively address inherent negatives stemming from the negative stakeholder operational footprint of their businesses. UPS and the Coca-Cola Company provide two examples to which we will return. Through its size and business model, UPS creates a large carbon footprint, which grows as its business expands: a classic example of an inherent negative. Recognizing this, the company has taken a variety of comprehensive actions to shrink its carbon footprint. As the world's largest beverage company and an iconic brand, Coca-Cola has long depended on the sales of its flagship brand, which became problematic as concerns over obesity and a healthy diet became widespread and when producing a Coke product requires vast amounts of water, a diminishing natural resource. By adjusting its product portfolio and its water resource management, the company is taking proactive actions to mitigate these inherent negatives.

Companies that strategically integrate these mitigating actions as a way of doing business—as part of their business model, rather than as incremental initiatives—are building resilient enterprises positioned to grow and remain competitive in this new social landscape of rising expectations and diminishing trust. To apply the Champion Brand model, these mitigating actions, at minimum, ensure *alignment* with stakeholder expectations and can, if taken further, become positive platforms that advance *authenticity, attachment,* and even *shared advocacy* with stakeholders.

However, inherent negatives extend beyond product attributes and operational supply chain management. They can also be embedded in corporate policies ranging from labor and human resources to governance, making them a C-suite management imperative. For example, companies like Facebook, Google, and Twitter operate at the epicenter of social media and the Internet, with their growth in active users, who pay no fee to use their products, directly linked to the companies' financial growth. The business model for these social media enterprises is to monetize the value of a growing, active user base in the form of advertising revenues, somewhat comparable to the Nielsen ratings used to measure the viewership of broadcast television shows. As the reach and scale of these businesses have grown pervasive, however, so has the potential for damaging stakeholder impact—providing a timely example of the dynamic of inherent negatives in action. The unprecedented global penetration of social media has sometimes outdriven management's understanding of the potential for negative stakeholder impact left in its wake—for example, fake news websites, the propagation of hate speech, or live videos of murders or suicides—leading to increasing public criticism of these businesses and demands for changes to the governance policies that steward these companies' business models.

Whatever their source, inherent negatives are embedded in the business model itself, ironically making them so ingrained that they sometimes go unnoticed when living inside the bubble of corporate culture. The consequences of that blind spot, however, can be substantial in this new era. Today, web-enabled stakeholders seeing the negative impact of an inherent negative through their outside-in lens have an unprecedented array of instant communications channels and social networks at their disposal to communicate their disapproval. If left unrecognized and unaddressed, a corporation's inherent negatives can become visible or viral well before it is prepared to constructively address them, potentially disrupting business strategies or—at the extreme— threatening its license to operate.

In fact, according to data from the Institute for Crisis Management, nearly 78 percent of business crises in 2015 were not due to sudden external events but due to smoldering issues that escalated to crises when they became public.[4] The degree of management control and responsibility is the key differentiator between sudden versus smoldering crises. While both categories of crises produce headlines, sudden crises are external events which are perceived as being beyond management control. Smoldering crises, the category in which inherent negatives belong, are perceived as being the responsibility and fault of a firm's leadership. "In extreme cases, and according to the Institute of Crisis Management database, it is in fact leadership decisions and actions that form the basis of most modern-day crises—not external threats or acts of God that we most frequently think of as a business crisis," explain Erika Hayes James and Lynn Perry Wooten.[5]

THE EMBEDDED FLIP SIDE

The flip side of an inherent negative can be construed as "shared value," a concept Michael Porter and Mark Kramer describe in their widely referenced 2011 *Harvard Business Review* article, "Creating Shared Value."[6] Like an inherent negative, a shared value resides at the core of the business model, but rather than negatively impacting stakeholders, a shared value builds economic success through strategies that create both financial and social value. In their article, Porter and Kramer point out that in the current climate of diminished trust in business, the more a business "embraces corporate social responsibility," the more a business is blamed for social problems. As "companies are perceived as profiting at the expense of the broader community," trust in business is caught in a cycle of diminished trust, divorced from society, which in turn leads to political policy that "undermines competitiveness." All of this is, in part, a result of businesses having fallen prey to a short-term perspective of creating short-term value and dismissing more sustainable strategies that consider a corporation's many stakeholders. The solution, according to Porter and Kramer, lies not so much in moving corporate social responsibility—which has become a primary vehicle for rebuilding trust—from the periphery to the center of contemporary business, but rather in a dramatic reconceptualization of corporate social responsibility which transforms it into creating shared value. Porter and Kramer state that what has typically been considered corporate social responsibility can be implemented in ways more relevant to a business's value proposition, thereby creating shared value, not merely short-term profit.

The concept of creating shared value epitomizes how much has changed in the rules of engagement between business and society from the previous era's accepted maxim that the mission of business is to maximize shareholder profits, with other societal benefits being ancillary offshoots:

> Companies must take the lead in bringing society and business back together. The recognition is there among sophisticated business and thought leaders, and promising elements

of a new model are emerging. Yet we still lack an overall framework for guiding these efforts, and most companies remain stuck in a "social responsibility" mind-set in which societal issues are at the periphery, not the core. The solution lies in the principle of shared value, which involves creating economic value in a way that also creates value for society by addressing its needs and challenges. Businesses must reconnect company success with social progress. Shared value is not social responsibility, philanthropy, or even sustainability, but a new way to achieve economic success.[7]

CODEPENDENCY

Porter and Kramer's shared-value framework, however, does not substantively address a critical dynamic for conducting business in the twenty-first century: the codependency of *both* mitigating risk *and* building brand under the ever-present watch of a global, web-empowered public. In today's context, a negative narrative previously visible to only a few can metastasize at warp speed, going "viral" on a global scale, creating a chronic drag on investments to build a corporate brand. A central implication of the inherent-negative model is that building upside brand achieves limited success without sufficiently managing downside risk from inherent negatives. Gone are the days when a company could simply rely on relationships built with a short list of academically credentialed key opinion leaders to serve as go-to third-party validators in traditional media to shield criticism of corporate actions that negatively impact stakeholders. Today, in addition to traditional key opinion leaders, communities of influence, particularly hyper-connected and engaged stakebrokers, can exponentially convert an emerging issue caused by an inherent negative into a global movement. When that happens, in the absence of both a credible track record of substantive actions to identify and address the inherent negatives of its business and a sustained, proactive engagement with stakeholders on those actions, a corporation's shared-value initiatives can be dismissed as cherry-picked goodwill efforts that conveniently bypass the critical thinking and strategic management required for balancing business needs with societal impact.

Consumer food companies, for example, can embrace a shared value by improving the efficiency and yields of cocoa farmers in Côte d'Ivoire, thereby improving both their companies' reliable supply of cocoa and the social and economic conditions for cocoa farmers and their suppliers. This example, profiled in Porter and Kramer's article, is clearly a win–win, a shared value. Despite that positive initiative, however, engaged stakeholders and stakebrokers continue to act as 24/7 watchdogs. Many are active critics of consumer food companies, seeing them as contributors to an epidemic in childhood obesity through, for example, misleading labeling, youth marketing practices, or creating products high in sugar, particularly high-fructose corn syrup and trans fats.

Porter and Kramer's shared-value article devotes only one sentence to the risk side of the dynamic interplay between risk mitigation and brand building: "Creating shared value presumes compliance with the law and ethical standards as well as mitigating any harm caused by the business, but goes far beyond that."[8] In their blog, as well as in their *California Management Review* article, Schulich Business School professors Andrew Crane and Dirk Matten cite this cursory treatment as one of "four big problems" associated with creating shared value. Referencing Porter and Kramer's sentence on risk, they state,

> Of course, this is where all those messy "trade-offs" are hiding. But as long as you can presume them away, you don't have to deal with them. In fact, there is only one sentence dedicated to the social harms, ethical norms and legal compliance in their whole article.[9]

For consumer food companies, a shared value at the heart of their business models would be a portfolio of delicious, healthy, and affordable food products, a quest many have been pursuing. As a predicate to that quest, however, most consumer food companies have recognized the codependency of risk mitigation and corporate brand building by proactively seeking to predict, discover, and address their businesses' inherent negatives, particularly in their supply chains and marketing policies. In some instances, an inherent negative—like the growth of sales for chocolate products putting a sustainable supply of cocoa at risk—can be converted into a source of shared value uniting multiple companies in an industry. For example, as expanding demand for chocolate from consumers in China and India has diminished cocoa supply, ten of the world's largest chocolate producers and cocoa processors agreed in 2014 to share data on farming practices to improve crop yields, an unprecedented move.[10] In this case, recognizing an inherent negative led to a common need among producers and ultimately a shared-value solution. In many instances, however, stakeholder impact from an inherent negative can simply be mitigated to reduce its impact.

Today, as with the insurance industry's theory of inherent vice, the failure to predict and mitigate an inherent negative can be devastating, making the sometimes hard work of identifying them a first-order priority for C-suite management. The transparency and velocity of action required of businesses in the twenty-first century have collapsed the boundaries, if there ever were any, between admirable and negative corporate behaviors in the minds of stakeholders. Concepts like shared value and corporate social responsibility are not in competition with each other, nor does the public accord "credits" for shared value and "debits" for negative impacts to derive a net corporate judgment, as though they were social accountants working with a new-age spreadsheet.

Instead, judgments are fluid. Corporate strategies that create shared value can positively elevate a corporate brand. To apply the Champion Brand framework, for example, shared-value solutions *align* with stakeholders, increasing their *attachment* to a product and company and positioning the company as both *authentic* and as a joint *advocate* with stakeholders for a public good. But if the public perceives the same company taking actions that advance their business while inflicting harm (an inherent negative), the business is fundamentally out of alignment with society, rendering their shared-value initiative *inauthentic*. Outrage will likely erupt quite visibly despite shared-value strategies.

"SO RIGHT AND YET SO WRONG"

Negative narratives have always traveled faster than positive ones (hence the old journalism maxim, "If it bleeds, it leads"), but today, bad news (even fake news) goes viral, making the business risk of inherent negatives even more substantial, which is why alignment lies as the threshold base of the Champion Brand pyramid. In addition, identifying or predicting what constitutes an inherent negative unaligned with stakeholder expectations can be challenging, exacerbated by the fundamental changes social media has brought about in the way the public consumes information. While some inherent negatives can be quickly identified, for example in supply chain operations, others can be more latent, perhaps hidden from a company's line of sight owing to a cultural blind spot but obvious to those impacted. In other instances, outrage from stakeholder damage, particularly on more nuanced issues, may be driven more by perception than fact, with negative commentary quickly reaching critical mass as a result of a lack of proactive corporate stakeholder engagement or timely social media monitoring to engage stakeholders before opposition hardens.

Nestlé provides an example that illustrates how inherent negatives addressed too slowly in this new landscape can create the potential for enduring criticism of a corporate brand, even one that has been widely recognized for its actions to advance sustainability and create instances of shared value. One of the world's largest, if not the largest, food and beverage company, Nestlé has been a consistent award winner for its policies, actions, and commitments to improve food security and sustainability and is considered to be one of the best places to work in Europe and Canada. In fact, Nestlé was among the top five highest-scoring brands in the 2014 Global Top 100 Champion Brands.[11]

Despite its laudable track record on shared value, Nestlé has a legacy of inherent negatives that persists. In the 1970s and 1980s, Nestlé's marketing of baby formula in economically depressed areas lacking secure access to clean water coincided with dramatic increases in childhood mortality compared with breastfed babies, triggering global boycotts of Nestlé products. Nestlé's initial response to the global criticism was to deflect the blame to the failure of others to ensure access to safe water. Critics later accused the company of promoting their branded bottled water as a solution.[12]

As a legacy of the outrage its actions engendered, two decades later in 2011, new Nestlé boycotts gained momentum in the Asia–Pacific region for Nestlé's promotion of breast milk substitutes, particularly for its marketing incentives to physicians and nurses to promote infant formula rather than breastfeeding, both less expensive than formula and widely viewed as a healthier alternative. As of 2013, the International Nestlé Boycott Committee has coordinated an ongoing international boycott, with the UK group Baby Milk Action serving as its secretariat.[13] The inherent negatives in this more recent boycott have not been with Nestlé's baby formula per se, but with Nestlé's marketing practices, both its promotions and the geographic target for its markets. While Nestlé has taken corrective actions, boycotts remain active.

During the recent multiyear drought in California requiring residents to cut water consumption by as much as 36 percent, Starbucks transferred its Ethos water bottling operations from California to Pennsylvania for the duration of the California drought on ethical grounds, taking action to address a negative stakeholder impact. In contrast, several companies, including Nestlé's Arrowhead and Pure Life brands, continued to source water in California for bottling, inciting more than five hundred thousand petitioners in 2015 to demand that Nestlé stop those operations.[14]

Several factors accelerated stakeholder outrage specifically targeted at Nestlé, without a comparable level of criticism leveled at other water bottlers in the state. First, Nestlé had only recently been required to pay a fee, $524 annually, for withdrawing water in San Bernardino National Forest, after operating for years on an expired permit, bottling water they sold for profit to citizens now living under drought restrictions.[15] In addition, Nestlé chairman Peter Brabeck-Letmathe had previously been widely criticized for dismissing access to water as a human right in a 2005 documentary, *We Feed the World*.[16] Following extensive criticism, Brabeck-Letmathe and Nestlé subsequently modified this position deeming access to water a human right, but links to his previous remarks periodically resurface on the Internet reigniting new criticism.[17]

Finally, as the issue in California escalated, the Nestlé Waters North America CEO, Tim Brown, was asked in a radio interview if he would ever consider moving the bottling operations out of California because of the drought. His answer: "Absolutely not. In fact, if I could increase it, I would."[18] Nestlé had facts to support this position, since bottled water ensures less wasted water. They also had a track record for their environmental stewardship to conserve water and a business case. The provocative content of Brown's remarks, however, implied a dismissive tone deafness for social context and stakeholders' expectations for businesses, similar to Mylan CEO Heather Bresch's comments on the EpiPen price increase. As an online science writer stated, "There's something absurd and immoral about a private company using as much water as they want while the rest of the state is facing severe restrictions."[19]

A similar seeming indifference to the social context of its water bottling operations erupted in the United States in 2016, as engaged stakeholders on social media became aware of Nestlé's planned plant expansion in Michigan, which had been making steady progress in state permitting. Despite Nestlé's commitment to investing $36 million in its Stanwood, Michigan, plant, its location, just 120 miles from Flint, sparked protests and boycotts since many Flint citizens still did not have access to clean tap water following the water crisis in that city that began in 2014. If the plant expansion had been approved, Nestlé would have nearly doubled the amount of groundwater pumped—and paying only $200 annually for access to the water. In the codependency between risk mitigation and brand building, the outrage generated made irrelevant any goodwill generated by Nestlé's globally recognized advances in sustainability and shared value. As one citizen put it, in writing to Michigan regulators, "Why on earth would the state of Michigan, given our lack of money to address water matters of our own, like Flint, even consider giving MORE water for little or no cost to a foreign corporation with annual profits in the billions?"[20]

Ironically, Nestlé is globally recognized for its leadership, specifically in terms of water resource management, fully embracing the tenets of creating shared value. Its status as a favored bull's-eye target for critics in the examples we have cited persists despite Nestlé's substantive actions to mitigate any negative impact from its bottled water operations. Instead, it reflects a corporate blind spot to sufficiently anticipate, respect, and address the social context for its bottling operations in an era characterized by a hyper-vigilant and empowered public.

Nestlé chairman and former CEO Paul Bulcke provided candid and thoughtful comments on the company's management of a different crisis involving its "Maggi" noodle brand in India. His remarks offer insight that could be applied to many corporations making the transition to doing business in this new landscape. The Maggi case involved a product ban imposed in 2015 after one of the government's laboratories found lead in a Maggi sample that greatly exceeded the permissible level. Ultimately, the High Court of Bombay ruled in Nestlé's favor overturning the ban, allowing Maggi sales to resume after three accredited labs confirmed the product's safety. But the financial damage from the five-month controversy, estimated at half a billion dollars, was considerable. Nestlé's dismissive reaction to regulators on the initial finding of lead irritated local officials, and its public silence when the story went viral allowed its critics to control the narrative. CEO Bulcke's lessons-learned reflections capture the new context for doing business in the twenty-first century:

> This is a case where you can be so right and yet so wrong. We were right on the factual arguments and yet so wrong on arguing. It's not a matter of being right. It is a matter of engaging in the right way and finding a solution. We live in an ambiguous world. We have to be able to cope with that.[21]

SHORT RAMP, BIG IMPACT, OBSTRUCTED VIEWS

For corporate C-suite management, the value of recognizing an inherent negative in advance, through the windshield rather than the rearview mirror, has never been greater. Today, new standards of transparency have transformed what was formerly a long lead time for an inherent negative to generate sufficient opposition to challenge corporate strategies. The fate of the tobacco industry is a classic example of the formerly long "ramp" for an inherent negative to gain momentum. Tobacco's inherent negative is a consequence of the product itself, a product that when used as intended can be fatal. Decades in the making, the evolving public perception about the consequences of *Mad Men*–style smoking finally created the rhetorical climate that forced the retro-chic habit out of the office and onto the sidewalks of office buildings.

Today, the dramatic changes in how people become informed—twice as many U.S. adults get their news online today than they do from newspapers, with 72 percent accessing news via mobile devices[22]—have made the lead time for an inherent negative to gain momentum very short. In addition, the urgent expectations for instant information now, with news items often shared thousands of times without sources being checked, and the emergence of fake news online, have made Mark Twain's comments from more than a century ago prescient: "A lie can travel half way around the work while the truth is putting on its shoes."

Anticipating inherent negatives in advance, through the windshield, has enormous business advantages over seeing them after they have erupted, through the rearview mirror.[23] A windshield view gives management time to assess the business and stakeholder impacts of potential actions, without controversy in which both traditional and social media, magnetically attracted to a dispute, quickly cause opinions to harden. When inherent negatives are recognized before they become a public "cause," stakeholders and critics are more amenable to working collaboratively to come up with a solution that works for both sides. Leveraging the lead time afforded by anticipating an issue through the windshield does not mean conducting secret discussions in closed-door negotiations, as though that were even an option in the ever-present transparency of the new social landscape. It does mean engaging with stakeholders to ensure a 360-degree insight into stakeholder impact, which is critical for avoiding both the insularity of the corporate bubble and the cultural blind spots from which no business is immune.

The business disadvantages of addressing inherent negatives through the rearview mirror after they have erupted are considerable: Business management must react quickly rather than plan proactively and may well face polarized critics, and media narratives can quickly solidify and amplify. In the current environment of media scrutiny, organized opposition, and increasing levels of transparency, boundaries between inherent negatives and nascent crises have become permeable. If most modern-day crises come from smoldering issues attributable to corporate leadership decisions and actions, what obstructs the view to see those issues in advance?

As Henry Mintzberg pointed out in his early work, time is the manager's most precious and fleeting asset.[24] This is truer than ever today, when every break in a meeting or conference—or family dinner—sees a scurry for smartphones. Urgencies of the here and now compete and often win against a common-sense desire to look ahead. If a manager does not have a full-blown crisis (in the traditional sense) on his or her hands, there are always pressing matters to attend to, with people and budgets already assigned. Uncommitted, discretionary funding reserved to address potential future contingencies is a business rarity. A decision to invest in mitigating an inherent negative, therefore, most likely means withdrawing funding from a competing initiative that has captured the energy of other executives in the company.

A more invidious reason to ignore or delay assessing a risk posed by an inherent negative is the tendency to underestimate critics, especially early critics, with a dismissive "What do they know?" Managers know their businesses, and they can be tempted to make an ad hominem attack on critics: They're just in it for money; their motives are suspect.

Actively resisting that perspective may be especially needed in industries that are science based or in which key customers share a similar knowledge base, thus creating an insular environment where it is easy to think, "We're doing just fine, thank you." Intel initially demonstrated this limited line of sight in the Pentium bug crisis by dismissing the issue because it felt that only theoretical mathematicians would be "bugged" by the bug. Like Nestlé's Paul Bulcke reflecting on the Maggi noodle controversy in India, Intel was both so right and so wrong.

This dismissal of critics has been duplicated by a kind of tech elite attitude of people who do not want to be bothered by such things as scooping up private consumer information when plotting maps, when criticized for substandard labor practices when manufacturing abroad, or when being accused of putting out fake news that influenced the 2016 U.S. presidential election. Doesn't the average person know these new tech giants have a higher calling? It becomes too easy to dismiss critics unless there is a corporate culture in place that allows people inside the corporation to say, "No, these critics are real. We ought to listen to what they have to say, and even engage with them to gather information."

An equally formidable obstacle to managing inherent negatives proactively through the windshield is a failure to understand an inherent negative's potential business impact. Some people will see an oncoming storm as just a blip on the radar screen, arguing that addressing a nascent problem only legitimizes the point and it would therefore be better to take no action. If we are quiet, they think, it will go away, but engagement legitimizes our critics and extends the story in the news cycle. As we will discuss in detail in chapter 6, Dow Corning recognized an emerging legal issue involving silicone breast implants, but the product's minor financial role in the company's overall business portfolio and the company's dismissal of the scientific legitimacy of claims, allowed the issue to escalate without substantive early intervention.[25] In the new world of around-the-clock news, even the concept of a "news cycle" has changed. The question is not whether to respond, but how to respond. Failure to identify and address critics in this environment leaves them with an unobstructed free kick at their goal.

ANTICIPATING INHERENT NEGATIVES

If the C-suite can get past the internal obstacles to acknowledging an inherent negative, the next question is, What methods can be used to see them in advance or judge their potential severity? How can C-suite management and corporate boards with their fiduciary responsibilities enhance their corporate risk assessment for doing business in the twenty-first century? And how can they assess the inherent negatives attached to prospective merger or acquisition targets, new market entries, new plant sites, or geographic expansions? In this new environment, systematically assessing the risk profile of the social landscape for current and prospective business strategies should be a prerequisite to making informed decisions, such as Shell is doing with their nontechnical risk assessment protocol.

Managing inherent negatives through the windshield requires a company to analyze the stakeholder impact of its products or services itself; assessing the full life cycle's stakeholder impact from upstream sourcing through downstream use and disposal; and assessing the stakeholder impact of corporate policies and governance, apart from the product or service itself. In conducting that analysis, guarding against the blinders of corporate cultural bubbles by gaining an understanding of different points of views is critical. If inherent negatives and the risks they pose were easy to anticipate and address, smoldering issues related to corporate leaders' decisions and actions would not be the predominant sources of corporate crises.

Instead, identifying inherent risks requires a concerted effort to expand a company's internal line of sight. Internally, developing a management culture that actively guards against the insularity of a corporate culture bubble starts at the top. CEOs and an executive team that actively and visibly seek out nonconforming points of view set the tone by modeling desired behavior and making diverse points of view politically safe within the culture. As Ram Charan counsels in *Owning Up*, C-suite management must actively assess the risks inherent to their business strategies. In the new social landscape, that means systematically integrating external perspectives into business management: operational monitoring (for example, monitoring stakeholder feedback through social media and customer relations and community advisory panels advising on the stakeholder impact of plant operations); issue management (for example, informed third-party input provided through mechanisms like advisory boards on priority issues like the Dow Chemical Company's Sustainability External Advisory Council[26]); and strategic planning (nontechnical risk assessments in the planning of potential capital investments, and integrating intelligence gained through direct stakeholder engagement mechanisms into the strategic planning process).

Finally, once identified, inherent negatives are addressed by taking action, which is institutionalized through changed business practices rather than individual initiatives. "Authenticity" has become a corporate buzzword, but its importance remains a reality. What a business does is the authentic content of what it says. Once a company identifies an inherent negative, position statements without actions are insufficient. Mitigating an inherent negative is not how a business changes its branding, although it may lead to a platform to help build a brand.

Waste Management provides an interesting example. Founded in 1971, Waste Management, Inc., has evolved from a garbage-hauling company to a waste management and environmental services company serving nearly twenty-seven million residential, industrial, municipal, and commercial companies in Canada, Puerto Rico, and the United States. In 2004, shortly after being named CEO, David Steiner and his management team, as leaders of the largest trash hauler in the United States, faced a challenge at the heart of its business model: Its customers were increasingly adopting the concept of zero waste. While good for the environment, zero waste was not a promising business proposition for a company whose growth depended on an increasing volume of the waste it hauled, treated, stored, and disposed of; an expanding source of waste was clearly an inherent negative at the core of Waste Management's business model. As Steiner commented to *Forbes* magazine in 2010,

> We know every American puts out 4.5 pounds of what we call "waste" every day. Our old model was to pick up waste and drop it in a landfill. But three years ago, our customers asked us, "How can you help us get to zero landfill?" Certainly, if you're a company reliant on your landfill network, zero landfill is a daunting thought.[27]

Under Steiner's leadership, the company transformed its business model, growing sales by helping its customers generate *less* waste and be smarter about the waste they did generate, with Waste Management diverting that waste through recycling, putting materials back into the product cycle, or extracting value from the waste itself. As of November 2016, the company's stock had nearly doubled over the previous five years, and the newly named CEO, James Fish, had committed to building on Steiner's legacy.[28]

UPS AND FACEBOOK

In some cases, a corporation's inherent negatives are embedded in the product or service itself, as illustrated by two very different examples: UPS and Facebook.

As a delivery company, UPS mitigates the negative impact of its carbon footprint through its single-network business model. UPS can optimize delivery efficiency, using technology and what they call an intermodal shifting strategy: the flexibility to shift the modes of transport for delivery in real time to reduce the energy consumed and the company's carbon footprint. While most customers know UPS through their familiar brown delivery trucks, 70 percent of the company's carbon footprint comes from elsewhere in its transit network.[29] An engineering company from its founding and enduring culture, UPS's strategies are driven by data-based efficiency. Its On-Road Integrated Optimization and Navigation (ORION) technology provides drivers with the most fuel-efficient routes and gives customers online and mobile access to track their deliveries and adjust preferences, including delivery locations and dates as needed. A decade in the making, ORION combines telematics with advanced algorithms to cut one hundred miles annually from UPS's deliveries, reducing its annual $CO2$ emissions by about one hundred thousand metric tons and reducing fuel consumption annually by ten million gallons.[30]

For the past few decades, rising stakeholder concerns regarding the impact of climate change and demands for sustainable products and services have encouraged many businesses to mitigate the inherent negatives in their operations that impact the environment and deplete natural resources, leading to triple-bottom-line reporting. UPS, which decided to issue its first corporate social responsibility report in 2001, takes that reporting a step further, integrating external third-party verification of its performance into its governance. Deloitte audits all of UPS's data; SGS, the world's leading inspection, verification, testing, and certification company, verifies its carbon data; and the Global Reporting Initiative, an independent standards organization, verifies the company's disclosures. "Such transparency presents more opportunities for us to improve," explains the UPS director of global sustainability, Steve Leffin, "and presents us the best opportunities as we measure, manage, and mitigate our impacts." Rather than an initiative, for UPS, mitigating its potential inherent negatives is fully integrated into its business model, its leadership, and governance.[31]

Controversies involving fake news on Facebook during the 2016 U.S. presidential election present another example of an inherent negative embedded in a product itself, although quite different from the case of UPS. As the number of Facebook users has grown into the billions, so has its advertising revenue. Facebook provides its advertisers with access to not only an enormous audience, but also to audience data and gives them the ability to target specific demographics. As the number of Facebook users grows, so do the data and demographics Facebook derives from the traffic running through its servers, which Facebook then can offer to its advertisers to target their ads and increase their potential impact.[32]

The user-friendly self-service advertising technology created by businesses like Facebook and Google has allowed businesses and entrepreneurs to easily set up a website, post ads, and create content that drives traffic to the account. In the Facebook business model, traffic, not the editorial quality of content, is king. What is critical is the degree of engagement— whether the content generates "likes," "shares," or comments.[33] In Facebook's business model, going viral is good for business, both for Facebook and for those creating content that drives traffic, even if the content is not true.[34]

Since negative news gains more traffic than positive news, in the business model underpinning the social media landscape, the incentive to be provocative, exaggerate, or just lie is an obvious outcome, even if unintended. A fabricated story regarding a dead FBI agent involved in the 2015–2016 Hillary Clinton e-mail controversy tallied more than five hundred thousand shares on Facebook. One version of a fake news story claiming Pope Francis had endorsed Donald Trump in the 2016 U.S. presidential election garnered more than nine hundred thousand Facebook shares. Fake news hoaxters during the election, including an enterprising teenager from Macedonia who wanted to find a way to make money, enjoyed a bonanza.[35]

The CEO of Facebook, Mark Zuckerberg, initially dismissed the thought that Facebook had grown to the point that it could influence an election as a "pretty crazy idea." However, building a business model by selling the pervasive reach of Facebook, with its data, to advertisers and then claiming that same reach was inconsequential was quickly rejected. One post on Twitter summed it up nicely: "Facebook is now in the awkward position of having to explain why they think they drive purchase decisions but not voting decisions."[36] As Facebook's user population has grown with a business model that monetizes traffic and engagement metrics, so has the potential inherent negative impact of fake news.

Zuckerberg has consistently maintained that Facebook is not a media company, stating that it is a neutral platform for connecting people: "We do not want to be arbiters of truth ourselves, but instead rely on our community and trusted third parties."[37] However, the reality is that Facebook's revenues grow through viral content, and Facebook's own social engagement metrics have demonstrated that viral fake news grows revenue both for Facebook and the content providers who gain revenue from advertisements on their sites. Ultimately, Facebook adopted a policy to mitigate the inherent negatives they had encountered: banning fake news sites from collecting funds through their advertising platforms. In addition, Facebook announced seven projects to stop the spread of misinformation among its users.[38]

In parallel with Facebook, Google's business model also allowed the company to benefit from viral fake news traffic. Its search advertising platform, Google AdWords, calculates advertising fees through clicks tied to key words rather than linked to the more in-depth engagement metrics involved with advertising on social media networks like Facebook. As the volume and velocity of clicks to access fake news grew, so did Google's revenues, since it is the dominant search engine and the leading source of traffic to media sites. Moving before Facebook in addressing this inherent negative, Google announced it would ban its digital ads from appearing on sites that "misrepresent, misstate or conceal information," giving its advertisers a clear incentive for accuracy.[39]

As a sign of things to come for corporations in the new frontier of social media, the CEO of PepsiCo, Indra Nooyi, also became a target of fake news. The news website Truth-Feed quoted her during the 2016 U.S. presidential election campaign as telling Trump supporters to "take their business elsewhere," causing PepsiCo stock to fall and prompting calls for a boycott. One problem: She never said it.[40]

UPSTREAM AND DOWNSTREAM

In addition to inherent negatives embedded in the policies governing a product or service itself, a corporation seeking to anticipate inherent negatives through the windshield should also understand the stakeholder impact of its supply chain or life cycle, both upstream (including issues such as sourcing raw materials and supplier management) and downstream (including issues such as usage and disposal). Increasing societal concerns related to sustainability have spurred many corporations to assess and address inherent negatives associated with their upstream supply chains. Projections on the declining global supply of upstream natural resources over the next fifteen years, for example, have made inherent negatives involving resource depletion linked with company growth untenable. As a United Nations Environment Programme report notes, "Corporate executives and board members owe it to their shareholders now to make critical choices that *decouple profitable growth from environmental impact and resource use,* to prepare for the economic reality of tomorrow, and to enable business to seize the scale of the opportunity."[41] A key factor in reaching the limit of capacity for natural resources is the projected doubling of the middle class by 2030, a projection reflected in the increasing cost of commodities that began around 2000 after a century of consistently falling prices.[42]

Coca-Cola's early identification and actions to address water stewardship and replacement provide a clear example of strategic actions to address an upstream inherent negative related to sustainability. Producing a given quantity of bottled Coke takes approximately four times as much water as what ends up in a bottle of Coke. Monetizing soft drinks in countries with shortages of drinkable water makes for a dramatic issue, particularly in India, which is experiencing increased groundwater depletion in some regions. Working with nongovernmental organizations, through water treatment plants and other means, Coca-Cola has committed to replacing the water it uses in its finished beverages, a goal for 2020 that the company met in 2015.[43]

Two implementation strategies—third-party engagement and third-party verification—have been critical to Coca-Cola's success in addressing its inherent negatives. While it may be natural and understandable for a company to react defensively or even combatively when its efforts to take constructive actions on inherent negatives go unacknowledged or even criticized, such reactions typically serve only to accelerate the criticism. Instead, engaging critics serves both to reduce outrage, and more importantly, can lead to new insights, getting the company outside of its corporate cultural bubble to develop a fuller understanding of the issue, particularly at a local level. "We've learned a great deal from the public challenges we've faced in India and other areas of water stress where we operate," explains Coca-Cola. "A lot of our learning has positively influenced the way we approach responsible water stewardship today, in India and elsewhere."[44] In addition, Coca-Cola not only internally monitors and measures the results of its actions but, like UPS, uses trusted and independent third parties to measure its results. Third-party validation is not a shield from criticism but a critical source of information for continuous improvement.

Inherent negatives, however, are not limited to issues of upstream supply chain and sustainability but also downstream uses that can further a potential negative impact. In this new age of Internet-enabled transparency, critics align with each other on very specific downstream issues in sophisticated ways. Take the issue of what might be called problem ingredients, which ranges from criticisms of toxic ingredients in clothing and antibiotics in food sources like poultry to accusations of chemicals causing endocrine disruption in cosmetic products. In some cases, the scientific basis for the accusations of potential harm is unsettled, particularly since proving a negative (that is, that no harm is being caused) is virtually impossible, and the functional benefit provided by the ingredients makes them difficult to replace in a product's manufacturing formulation. As web-savvy activists have discovered, the more effective path to eliminating what they consider a problem ingredient from products is to target the downstream consumer-brand products that contain the ingredient, rather than focus on the upstream producer of the chemical. The more consumer products sold with the ingredient, they argue, the greater the potential harm; thus, activists seek to create de facto market-based bans rather than waiting for regulatory forces, scientific consensus, or even a courtroom. It is a page out of Naomi Klein's *No Logo*.

The movement for safe cosmetics, in which activists have targeted the elimination of chemicals called phthalates and bisphenol A (BPA) produced by chemical manufacturers provides an example. In a pacifier, phthalates make the rubber soft. This group of chemicals is also used in personal care products like nail polish, household cleaners, and food packaging. Activists critical of phthalates for their potential link to endocrine disruption in humans and animals, particularly reptiles, learned that targeting downstream consumer-branded products using the chemicals—L'Oréal, Maybelline, and Revlon—was a faster track to eliminating them than attacking upstream chemical producers. Through web-empowered social media, critics of phthalates have fostered consumer unrest about the ingredients, seeking downstream phthalate-free consumer product formulations, even while the scientific basis for the critics' claims is still a matter of considerable debate.

Activists have used a similar approach to raise concerns that poultry producers' use of the same antibiotics used to treat human illnesses in poultry feedstock to accelerate weight gain increases the risk of creating drug-resistant bacteria in humans. This issue is a classic inherent negative: As poultry consumption has grown globally, so has the human health risk posed by this practice. And, unlike the phthalate debate, the use of antibiotics in poultry feedstock is a concern with scientific consensus. Having spread enough concern to have a ban on this practice implemented in Canada and Europe, the practice is still legal in the United States, driving increasing activism targeting not only U.S. poultry producers but also downstream fast-food restaurants to source antibiotic-free poultry.

Anticipating inherent negatives through the windshield also requires a thorough understanding of use and disposal. Diageo, whose brands include a range of well-known spirit brands, proactively and creatively manages downstream issues resulting from the consumption of its products. Unlike tobacco, which when used as intended can be fatal, spirits can be harmless when consumed responsibly, but the potential for harm is inherent in its downstream use—an inherent negative that Diageo fully acknowledges: "Alcohol can be part of a balanced lifestyle when consumed moderately and responsibly by adults who choose to drink, and can play a positive role in social occasions and celebrations. However, we recognize that harmful drinking creates problems for individuals and society."[45]

Rather than a strategy of incremental initiatives, Diageo has integrated the responsible downstream use and consumption of its products into its corporate governance and policies. The Diageo Marketing Code, reviewed every twelve to eighteen months, governs the company and the third parties with whom it partners and is applied to all corporate activities, from research and development to marketing, promotion, and packaging. Its programs to address consumption include training bartenders, educational programs for the responsible use of its products, and directly engaging with the concerns of groups such as Mothers Against Drunk Driving (MADD). To address drunk driving in advance of the 2016 holidays, Diageo launched an immersive virtual reality experience called "Decisions," putting consumers in the virtual front seat of a vehicle involved in a drunk-driving collision. This move was described as an industry first in the spirits trade.[46]

The potential for the downstream misuse of alcohol products at least has the benefit of history to alert companies in the spirits businesses to the potential risk of inherent negatives. In the new frontier of social media, downstream end-user usage is making history as we watch, sometimes complicating the ability to foresee what can go wrong and inventing creative ways to address an issue, once identified. Hate speech presents a timely example. The more social media platforms like Facebook and Twitter expand, the greater is the potential for misuse by downstream users to cause harm. Unlike the issue of fake news, hate speech does not necessarily financially benefit social media companies unless the hate speech itself gains a viral level of magnitude, driving traffic and ad revenue (no matter how unintended). Instead, the impact from hate speech has become a national security issue, as terrorists exploit social media platforms for recruitment. And, in countries like Germany where hate speech is illegal, addressing it becomes a matter of compliance. In October 2016, the German minister of justice, Heiko Maas, threatened that Facebook and Twitter could be held criminally liable if they did not remove hate speech content more quickly.[47] Within the United States, the First Amendment to the United States Constitution largely protects such expression, but when the speech crosses the line to threatening an identifiable individual, organization, or institution, it becomes criminal conduct and is not protected.

Claiming that social media companies cannot be held responsible for hate speech content created by its downstream users is an argument that might have worked in a previous era, but is untenable as societal expectations for business have grown. Facebook has outpaced Twitter in addressing this inherent negative with some creative approaches. Its Online Civil Courage Initiative employs the power of Facebook's pervasive reach to empower its users to fight back against racist trolls and violent extremists on the Internet. Working with more than eighty activist groups and nongovernmental organizations in France, Germany, and the United Kingdom since January 2016, Facebook is expanding the Initiative's network to more regions, providing advertising credits, marketing resources, and strategic support to anti-hate activist groups.[48]

Twitter has been slower off the mark to mitigate hate speech, a downstream inherent negative in its business model. Because Twitter allows anonymity, it has been a hate-speech magnet, and its size, unlike that of other sites allowing anonymity, magnifies its potential for harm. While Twitter users have reported abuses, the company initially offered few tools for users to screen unwanted content in the first place. The hate-speech campaign against *Ghostbusters* star Leslie Jones made Twitter's problem with hate speech so visible that it was cited as one of the main reasons the software company Salesforce decided not to acquire it. Late in 2016, Twitter announced new feature to give users more control, including keyword filtering to block offending tweets and retraining support staff and adding internal staff tools to deal with abuse incidents.[49]

Corporations that have integrated inherent negatives related to sustainability and corporate social responsibility into their strategic management and governance, as opposed to considering them separate, incremental initiatives, have substantially advanced their strategic risk management for doing business in the twenty-first century, a century beginning with a large trust–expectations gap. Inherent negatives, however, are not limited to issues of sustainability, as many of the examples in this chapter illustrate. Particularly with new business models, as with social media, inherent negatives may be hard to foresee and can arrive without the benefit of precedents on how to address them. As additional new technologies like artificial intelligence, nanotechnology, driverless cars and trucks, and virtual reality become mainstream elements of products in commerce and as the Internet of things integrates Wi-Fi into a vast array of products, due diligence in predicting and addressing inherent negatives will become even more imperative, as will the creative thinking to anticipate scenarios to address them. Predicting risk, the premise that began this chapter as the enabling basis for the modern form of business, is not going to get any easier.

4

CORPORATE CHARACTER

In the instantly transparent world of the new social landscape, all aspects of what constitutes a corporation's identity are under unprecedented scrutiny from web-enabled stakeholders—both external and internal—ready to pounce when words and actions do not align. A corporation's character becomes the sum of its beliefs, vision, values, words, and actions and drives its reputation. To borrow an observation from Abraham Lincoln, a tall man who would cast a long shadow, "Perhaps a man's character is like a tree, and his reputation like its shadow; the shadow is what we think of it; the tree is the real thing."

The surest mitigation of reputational risk for conducting business in the twenty-first century is a corporate character grounded in behavior that withstands internal and external stakeholder scrutiny making corporate character a strategic governance priority for executive management and boards of directors. Like Lincoln's tree analogy, corporate character is the "real thing": how an organization behaves in society, how it expresses itself, and how it engages internally and externally. It is the combination of an organization's authenticity, culture, and predictable behavior consistent with the organization's vision and values that engenders trust through multiple and changeable channels of communications and engagement.

Today, corporate character is observed, tested, and judged through every stakeholder's interaction with any employee, with negative experiences quickly posted online with the potential to go viral, particularly if captured visually. Every employee, not just the executive office, stewards the organization's corporate character.

"I MUST RESIGN FROM THIS ONCE GREAT COMPANY"

The new social landscape has reset the social contract for what constitutes an acceptable corporate character. Equally distinctive of this new era is the real-time global visibility of that character in action, particularly when a company's vision and values do not match its words or actions. Traditionally, for example, corporate CEO pronouncements have represented the voice of the company, with those words sometimes ignored by employees busy with their own lives and work. CEOs at IBM and Oracle discovered just how much things had changed following the election of Donald Trump as president of the United States. IBM CEO Ginni Rometty's public letter to then-president-elect Trump posted on November 15, 2016, articulated several ideas and initiatives that "represent ways we can work together" while also acknowledging there would likely be issues in the coming years on which IBM and the Trump administration would disagree.

A few days later, IBM digital strategist Elizabeth Wood posted a public letter of resignation to Rometty on her LinkedIn profile and Twitter feed, which then became national news. "Your letter," wrote Wood, "offered the backing of IBM's global workforce in support of his [Trump's] agenda that preys on marginalized people and threatens my well-being as a woman, a Latina, and a concerned citizen." She also criticized the inconsistencies between Rometty's letter to Trump and IBM's recruitment material, which declares that the company's future depends on realizing "an inclusive and welcoming culture." While Rometty referenced diversity and tolerance in an e-mail to employees regarding her letter to President-elect Trump, she omitted those topics in her actual letter to Trump, which Ms. Wood declared a "huge disservice."[1]

In a similar scenario, Oracle employee George Polisner posted on LinkedIn his resignation letter to the Oracle CEO, Safra Catz, in protest of her decision to join Trump's transition team, an action taken without an explanation given to employees. "I am not with President-elect Trump," Polisner wrote, "and I am not here to help him in any way. In fact when his policies border on the unconstitutional, the criminal, and morally unjust I am here to oppose him in every way possible. Therefore, I must resign from this once great company."[2]

Just a few years ago, similar employee dissatisfaction would more likely have been voiced over lunch or after-work drinks, and a friendly debate among colleagues might have ensued. At most, the conversation would have made the organizational grapevine. Today, these protests are newsworthy events and, just as significantly, reach the level of resigning from a company based on a misalignment of values and principles between employee and employer. Escalating expectations for the role of business in society have reframed employees' relationships with their employers.

To illustrate the magnitude of this change, consider that the concept of corporate identity, as previously understood and discussed in business literature and business schools, had its origins in the more tactical realm of visual identity or, put more simply, the corporate logo. Some firms, for example, the brand consulting firm Landor in the United States, remain specialists in visual identity. A quick look at Landor's website reveals the extent to which this one agency is responsible for the visual expressions of so many well-known corporations, from airlines to package delivery firms, and for so many of the images we encounter in everyday life. In and of itself, visual identity is no small thing, from the red Spencerian script of Coca-Cola or the round GE "meatball" to name two venerable images, to the more recent Apple logo of an apple with a bite taken out of it and the colorful letters of Google. Famous and successful logos that identify major companies play a role in engaging a company's stakeholders. In the age of Instagram and Snapchat, a resonant visual representation of a large organization connects with stakeholders instantaneously.

FROM CORPORATE IDENTITY
TO CORPORATE CHARACTER

Although an organization's visual identity can be the most conspicuous aspect of its identity, the concept of corporate character goes further. Wally Olins, a pioneer of corporate branding, suggested that an organization is both understood and manifested through four vectors or transmitters: products and services, environments, communications, and behavior.[3] The first three vectors, Olins felt, are observable, whereas behavior is one that you can feel, experience, and almost see. Olins later asserted that the balance of these four vectors is rarely equal. According to Olins, this broader definition of an organization's identity, consisting of the four vectors, determines how it is perceived by society. Olins argued that corporate identity was more than tactical nomenclature or visual identity systems. Instead, the four vectors together strategically define how the company projects its culture, vision, and values both externally and internally.

The American catalogue company L.L.Bean provides a good example for understanding an organization's identity through its products. In 1912, hunters in New England often wore waterproof rubber boots, which would get sweaty, or leather boots, which would get wet. As a solution to these problems, a man named Leon Leonwood Bean sewed the rubber bottom from a working boot to the top of a leather hunting boot and began to sell the boot through a mail-order catalogue. Early twentieth-century catalogue shoppers faced a hesitation barrier similar to that faced by early Internet adopters reluctant to pay for online purchases with a credit card. Shoppers accustomed to trusting shoe quality by first trying on a shoe were reticent to buy shoes through a catalogue. From this concern came Bean's 100 percent guarantee—a good thing since some of Bean's early boots fell apart.

The catalogue changed with the times. As hiking and outdoor recreation grew in popularity during the 1970s, demand for the latest synthetic outerwear more than rivaled demand for the old-fashioned wool shirts and jackets favored by earlier generations. As individual items were discontinued, no doubt for sound business reasons, L.L.Bean began to resemble a retailer of mid-market leisure clothing more so than an outdoor outfitter. Some items, like the boots, moccasins, and a Norwegian-style fisherman's sweater became popularized by the tongue-in-cheek reference guide *The Official Preppy Handbook*. But as the company's product portfolio evolved, for a time even the Norwegian sweater disappeared (recently coming back at a sufficient markup). Today, a signature line reprises slimmed-down "classics" with a sufficient amount of clothing for outdoor use, if perhaps primarily suited to birders and meteorologists on the Weather Channel. For the past few holiday seasons, the outdoors look has become so popular that the hunting shoe, long renamed the L.L.Bean duck boot (branding for the squeamish?), has been sold out and backordered, remaining the catalogue's centerpiece. Recognizing the urban appeal of this backwoods fashion icon, in 2017 L.L.Bean for the first time introduced limited edition duck boots in various colors, with the warning that "once they're gone, they're gone."[4] The brick-and-mortar L.L.Bean store itself, a frequent stop for hunters and fishers on the way to down-east Maine, still sells canoes and kayaks.

Can L.L.Bean be said to retain its differentiated identity linked to hunting and fishing as its product portfolio has evolved over time? This is a bit of an ephemeral issue, but the 100 percent guarantee is still in place. Today, L.L.Bean customer service employees monitoring online customer reviews of their products proactively engage in online conversation to offer a free replacement when a customer review calls out a purchased product that does not perform as advertised, with the tangible evidence of the 100 percent guarantee fully visible to anyone browsing the comments section.

Olins's environment vector might play a more significant role for a hotel chain. A Ritz-Carlton lobby conveys an identity substantially different from that of a Holiday Inn Express. Although a Ritz-Carlton experience may not include convenient access to an interstate highway, their white gloves likely do not tarnish the entry door's polished brass handles. The Ritz-Carlton "passion for perfection" ethos is introduced in the orientation process, reinforced through training, reviewed daily in the line-up, and practiced by everybody in the organization.

Coca-Cola provides perhaps the quintessential example of a company's identity being transmitted through the vector of communications. Whether it is the iconic red, Spencerian script of the product name, or the catchy tune, Coca-Cola has been identified with refreshment since the late 1800s. As Olins pointed out, all fast-moving consumer goods are primarily driven by communication, and more specifically, advertising.

Of Olins's four identity vectors, behavior may be the most significant. Olins suggested that how an organization behaves is not limited to its actions in the marketplace, but also includes how it treats its employees. In his 2003 work, *On Brand*, Olins explained "why brands are important inside companies."[5] In fact, in today's new social landscape, the role of an organization's employees has become ever more integral. To what extent does an employee identify with his or her company? This question has become more common, as the demands of productivity and globalization—the usual suspects—have eroded a previous generation's not unreasonable expectation to spend a career with, and climb the corporate ladder of, a single company.

COLLAPSING INTERNAL AND EXTERNAL BOUNDARIES

How a company's character is perceived, its "shadow" to apply Lincoln's analogy, affects both internal and external stakeholders. *Fortune* naming Whole Foods Market as the best company to work for cheers up employees, who in turn act cheerfully at work, which in turn makes for a better experience for customers, who then decide it is worth paying a bit more for a pleasant experience and better quality. Business calls this a virtuous circle. Even this virtuous circle, however, can be disrupted when changes in the shape of the "tree" (that is, the real thing) also change the shape of the "shadow."

As a series of widely shared scandals about Whole Foods grew online—overcharging by overstating the weight of prepackaged goods; selling asparagus soaked in water for $6; using residents of a Colorado rehabilitation program to make some of its high-priced products—the company became a source for late-night comedy and acquired the online nickname of "Whole Paycheck," which earned an entry in the online dictionary of slang words and phrases Urban Dictionary. As the changed narrative for Whole Foods gained online momentum, a growing cadre of online detectives publicly debated the truth or fraud involved in a feud between Whole Foods and a customer who had accused the store of decorating a cake he ordered with an anti-gay slur in hand-lettered icing.[6]

The experience of Whole Foods provides a classic example of why corporate character in the twenty-first century's new social landscape is a strategic governance imperative for executive management and boards of directors. Whether the criticisms leveled at Whole Foods were based on verifiable flaws in operations (which has subjected Whole Foods to fines and regulatory warnings) or whether Whole Foods is the victim of a fraud, the visible and persistent online scrutiny of the company's corporate character has eroded its value to shareholders. By early 2017, the cumulative impact from these incidents shared online was its stock trading at less than 50 percent of the ten-year high it had reached in 2013, which perhaps added to the reasons Amazon targeted it for acquisition.

Nearly every large company has a set of values, core beliefs, or principles, but it is quite likely that an employee might have to look them up to see what they are. Training sessions inculcating principles that are at odds with an employee's experience are not simply unhelpful, but in the new social landscape are likely to become a public discussion about the company's character. In their 1997 article, "A European View on Corporate Identity: An Interview with Wally Olins," Majken Schultz and Mary Jo Hatch wrote that at one time, an organization could maintain a boundary between its internal operations and its external activities. However, this compartmentalization of tasks was now breaking down in response to increased demands to integrate functions across an organization, such as marketing, human resources, public relations, engineering, and production, to help differentiate a company from its global competition.[7]

If the boundaries between internal and external activities were blurring in the late 1990s, as Schultz and Hatch observed, those boundaries have evaporated in the twenty-first century. Employees and external stakeholders publicly audit how a company's actions, strategies, and operations align with its values and vision, as the IBM, Oracle, and Whole Foods examples demonstrate.

A company's character has become the sum of how a company does business, with its employees and external stakeholders acting as its perpetual public auditors.

The positive public perception of Johnson and Johnson may well have roots in its well-known credo which its Chairman Robert Wood Johnson wrote in 1943 just prior to the company becoming publicly traded. The credo literally defines how Johnson and Johnson does business in comprehensive, clear, and specific language to the point where the credo can be translated into a basis for decision making. Johnson and Johnson managers say that ten minutes into a company meeting, someone will ask if what is being proposed is consistent with the credo. To be sure, the modern Johnson and Johnson is a large pharmaceutical company that has carefully associated the company with "moms, babies, and Band-Aids" through ad campaigns like "A baby changes everything." Still, the credo inspires a culture where a national shortage of nurses is met with the company's offer to pay tuition for nursing school. Actions retain a level of plausibility as they are aligned with the credo, and this is made possible by a remarkable culture. Johnson and Johnson calls its script logo the "trust mark."

Johnson and Johnson is unusual in its relationship with its employees, as made clear in its credo, which demonstrates how a company's clearly stated obligations to stakeholders affects its corporate culture and perception. The company's commitment to physicians, nurses, and those who use its products and services—the first stakeholder group discussed in the credo—led to its scholarship program for nursing degrees. Citing employees as the credo's key second stakeholder group is not an overly ambitious claim when considering how direct a role internal stakeholders play in corporate culture and the corporate character that culture represents.

UPS provides another example of a company with a pervasive employee understanding of how it does business. In addition to its proactive initiatives to mitigate the inherent negatives of its business, UPS's strong commitment to and observable track record of promoting from within preserve an operational heritage well understood by its more than four hundred thousand employees. As the current CEO, David Abney, has commented, UPS has not just been a job or career, "It's a way of life." When UPS named Abney's predecessor, Scott Davis, to the CEO slot, business media speculated that Abney and other senior leaders might seek a promotion for the top job at another company. However, jumping to another company is not part of UPS's DNA. "We focus on promotion from within and giving people opportunities and it's amazing to see people grow and develop over the years," explains Abney.[8]

PIVOTAL EMPLOYEE STAKEHOLDERS

In fact, as corporations have begun to recognize the implications of the widening gap between declining trust and rising expectations for business, employee engagement and communications have increasingly become strategic priorities and critical factors in addressing corporate character. In the new social landscape, stakeholder "wheel" models placing top management at the hub as a frame to discuss business strategies and ethics have become less and less conceptually useful. This is not to discount the role of leadership and responsibility of top executives. In terms of corporate character, it is to say that seeing top executives as existing in a separate sphere from the organization ignores the reality of a new organizational ecosystem. In this new ecosystem, a key factor is the *relationship* between top management and employees, and seeing employees as an opportunity for investment, rather than as a cost, can only enhance an authentic corporate character in which corporate vision is shared. We suggest this not as idealistic or theoretical concepts but as something that, owing in part to the influence of the Internet and social media, is simply becoming the fact of the matter.

Take the example of the employee blog. When blogging first became popular, a good deal of corporate hand-wringing took place over what guidelines management should provide to employees for blogging so that a company would not be embarrassed or have inside information shared externally. There is an argument to be made for this, including the need to provide some sense of security for employee bloggers to understand what is in bounds. But the reality is, just as the new social landscape has evaporated the boundaries between internal and external, rigid lines between discrete classification of stakeholders have been erased. Employees are also consumers, activists, and investors. In this new context, as many companies have discovered, the best answer is to cultivate an organization in which what an employee says in public or on the web is not something to worry about. A sufficient level of buy-in, to use an older management term, allows employees to further the aims of the organization.

Just as important, eroding trust in business has meant that word of mouth, personal experiences, and employees are more trusted "voices" for business than top management or official spokespeople. That does not mean senior management statements are irrelevant. But unlimited access to vast sources of information now provides an unprecedented context for anyone to assess what senior management says.

Senior management statements are now judged, in real time, on how consistently their words align with the actions a company has taken and with how consistently they align with what nonmanagement employees say, given the countless communications paths now open to anyone who wants to talk or engage.

The role of Facebook's employees in CEO Mark Zuckerberg's evolving position on fake news is a timely example. As widely reported in a variety of media, Facebook employees reacted to Zuckerberg's initial dismissive response to the idea that fake news shared on Facebook affected the outcome of the 2016 U.S. presidential election by forming an unofficial task force, including employees from across the company.

The online social news platform BuzzFeed reported that employees, speaking anonymously after being warned by management not to speak to the press, met secretly to develop recommendations for Facebook management. "It's not a crazy idea. What is crazy is for him [Zuckerberg] to come out and dismiss it like that, when he knows, and those of us at the company know, that fake news has run wild on our platform during the entire campaign season," said one Facebook employee from its social networking division. Similarly, a former Facebook designer, Bobby Goodlatte, posted on his Facebook wall, "Sadly, News Feed optimizes for engagement. As we've learned in this election, bullshit is highly engaging. A bias towards truth isn't an impossible goal. Wikipedia, for instance, bends toward the truth despite a massive audience. But it's clear that democracy suffers if our news environment incentivizes bullshit."[9]

As discussed in chapter 3, Facebook has taken steps to mitigate the inherent negatives in its business model that can incentivize fake news. The key point here is the strategic roles employees, and their relationship with top management, have played in creating the context to trigger Facebook's course correction on this issue, played out for the public to see. The reality of fake news and management's initial reaction to it struck at the heart of Facebook's corporate character and could not be ignored.

At the customer or consumer level, tech companies have seemed to defy the gravity of what should be dents to their reputation. Apple can appear on the front page of the *New York Times* for building devices in China and then tell a sitting U.S. president that employment in America is not an issue that concerns them. And while their batteries may be sometimes problematic, since 2011 the company has maintained the top spot in brand equity rankings, until falling to number 2 in 2017.[10] Google might zap up consumer information while mapping suburban streets or comply with some levels of censorship in China, but in 2017 it displaced Apple for the top ranking in brand equity. Banner ads related to your last purchase that follow you around on any web search (which recalls the "futuristic" film *Minority Report*) do not seem to cause much of a stir and certainly not a product boycott. The power of consumer convenience, a kind of consumer populism and, of course, cachet, have afforded these companies a Teflon coating. But for Facebook employees, the company's initial position on fake news crossed a values line that had to be addressed.

COMPETING FOR THE NEXT GENERATION

Another factor driving the growing strategic importance of a corporation's employee engagement and communications has been the recruitment and retention of employees. This is particularly the case for millennials (those born from the early 1980s to the mid-1990s), who in 2015 became the largest share of the American workforce,[11] and for Generation Z (those born since 1996) who will represent 40 percent of all consumers by 2020.[12] Corporate character will be a high priority for the next generation of corporate leaders, who tend to be more loyal to core values than to a particular company, making corporate character central to recruitment and retention initiatives. Deloitte's 2016 survey of millennials, for example, found that 88 percent of those remaining in the company for more than five years reported sharing the organization's sense of purpose. For those leaving the company within two years, alignment with the sense of purpose fell to 63 percent.[13] As a participant in a 2016 Institute for Public Relations study explained,

> With these new generations coming into the workforce, more than ever they are looking for those values. That's important to them. What does a company stand for, what does it mean? So, we're seeing companies put a lot more time, effort and resources into communicating and living their values and that is true from employee orientation from the beginning. . . . It's true in recruiting as they try to find people who match their values, in new employee orientation and then throughout that lifecycle.[14]

With the global recession hitting them at the start of their careers, millennials may be the first generation to believe they will not retire better off than their parents, a long-held American cultural expectation. Data show good reason for that anxiety. An analysis of Federal Reserve data by the advocacy group Young Invincibles shows that millennials are earning 20 percent less than boomers at the same stage of life.[15]

Recognizing this disparity, Starbucks has partnered with Arizona State University to offer American full- and part-time employees without a four-year degree (who make up 70 percent of the Starbucks workforce) full tuition for an online undergraduate degree program.[16]

Boxed, an e-commerce startup competitor to wholesale clubs like Costco and Sam's Club, is similarly offering to pay the college tuition of its employees' children through a nonprofit foundation created and funded by its CEO, Chieh Huang. Referring to the company's nearly one hundred U.S. warehouse workers, Huang explained why this benefit was a better solution than a higher salary: "There is an issue of inequality of opportunity. If you can barely afford a car and then you get a double salary, maybe you can afford a car. But can you really pay four years of education for your children?" When some workers texted their spouses with the news, the response from one spouse was "You can never leave this company ever." As Huang explained, "These folks have dedicated themselves to our company day in and day out. I'm really nothing without them, so this was just my way of making the situation right."[17]

Absent from the explanations of employee policies like these is competitive labor data on salaries. Instead, the rationale is that it is the right thing to do, both for the companies and for society as a whole.

AN ALWAYS-ON CHARACTER AUDIT

In the new social landscape, corporate character is a key fiduciary responsibility of executive management and boards of directors, as the alignment of corporate strategies with a company's values is under persistent internal and external scrutiny. The Danish firm Lego, which took its name from the Danish for "good learning," provides a fitting example. The largest toy manufacturer in the world, Lego has extended its brand through its own movies, theme parks, books, and video games. However, a 2016 study documenting "significant exponential increases in violence over time" in Lego toys garnered global visibility because changes in Lego's product portfolio did not align with the "shadow" of its perceived corporate character. Lego had a history of differentiating itself through its nonviolent toys: "There is, in this nervous world, one toy that does not shoot, go boom or bang or rat-a-tat-tat," a 1966 Lego ad reads. "Its name is Lego. It makes things." Compared to competitors, the study acknowledged, Lego's toys "could still be considered relatively mild," and Lego's brand manager explained that the company distinguishes between "conflict" and "violence."[18] That nuanced distinction was missed by the many online articles and comments surprised by the incongruity between what was understood to be Lego's corporate character and its evolving product strategies.

The history behind Nike's "swoosh" logo, which has adorned the clothing of superstar athletes more than once (just think of Tiger Woods's cap and shirt) was particularly fortuitous. Rather than consult a large design firm and numerous focus groups, Nike purchased its logo from a local artist for a sum that would not keep a teenager in sneakers for a season, and this became part of the story of the company's origins.[19] A particularly fortuitous or historically resonant logo or tagline suggests a larger narrative. However, before Nike took extensive constructive actions to improve the labor conditions of its offshore clothing suppliers, the swoosh at the bottom of college sweatshirts for some students meant sweatshops, not "Just do it." By taking seriously the damaging independent report on labor conditions involved with its clothing production and institutionalizing corrections, Nike addressed a sourcing strategy that had raised questions about its corporate character. Once those issues were substantively addressed, Nike could return to building the upside of its brand. If Nike had ignored the inherent negative in its upstream supply chain, would Reebok have remained a more serious contender in the sneaker brands' battle for cool? Would consumers now be moving in greater numbers to the fast-growing Baltimore upstart Under Armour?

A brand like Nike's can become the kernel of a narrative that accrues in meaning to represent corporate character: a symbol of offshore labor exploitation (low-cost offshore labor was, after all, part of Nike co-founder Phil Knight's original business plan) or, having sufficiently mitigated its most high-profile inherent negative, a symbol of heritage in the ongoing story of a young innovator founding a company that continues to endorse the most popular sports stars of the moment and supports efforts aimed at inclusive athletic participation such as Title Nine.

As Nike illustrates, preserving the heritage of corporate character and the considerable value it engenders, both internally and externally, is an ongoing fiduciary management responsibility requiring active stewardship. It is not about wordsmithing corporate vision and values statements that then lie dormant. Instead, it is about fully integrating a company's vision and values with its business decisions on strategies and policies. Now, more than ever before, doing business requires executive leaders who model the stewardship of corporate character, asking uncomfortable, even inconvenient, questions about the alignment between a company's vision and values and its business strategies and policies as a way of doing business. Perhaps even more important, to build an internal culture that reflects the company's character, executive leaders must visibly reward and recognize employees who audit that alignment and flag strategic inconsistencies and make it politically safe for them to do so. As the many examples in this and other chapters illustrate, it is better to correct course before a divergence from vision and values becomes newsworthy, goes viral, and then must be managed through the rearview mirror, not the windshield.

It is not so much inconsistency per se that erodes corporate character. Companies, like people, make mistakes. Rather, it is the failure to recognize and correct the business decisions that diverted an organization from it vision and values that erodes character.

The Danish pharmaceutical company Novo Nordisk provides a case in point. The company's stated purpose is to prevent, treat, and ultimately cure diabetes, "but also improve the lives of those living with other serious chronic conditions."[20] The "Novo Nordisk Way" is a guiding principle for how the company works, but the company lost its way when it decided to join a multiparty court case against the South African government in 2001, fighting the government's importation and production of inexpensive medications for patients with HIV and AIDS. That business decision prompted protests against the company for the inconsistency between the lawsuit's arguments and the company's stated mission. The company corrected course, withdrawing from the lawsuit and subsequently openly declaring that the litigation was a major mistake that was inconsistent with its values.[21]

In today's vernacular, such course corrections, fully disclosed, become teachable moments in building and stewarding corporate character. They become visible not only owing to today's always-on, transparent environment, but also because behaviors like a business openly disclosing a mistake and making a course correction are unexpected. Such actions are counterintuitive to the big-business stereotype cultivated and hardened through periods of long-standing, pervasive distrust.

Your stereotype walks through the door before you do. Whether applied to a person or a business, a stereotype inevitably acts as a prism filtering how words and actions are interpreted. Ironically, the combination of the pervasive distrust for business and high expectations for its role in society may have created an opportunity: Businesses that disrupt the stereotype of distrust through actions that demonstrate a corporate character capable of withstanding internal and external scrutiny can become headline news.

Just ask the CEO of Patagonia, Rose Marcario, whose 2015 customer holiday message lit up the web when she suggested customers *not* buy new Patagonia clothes for the holiday but fix their old ones instead: "As individual consumers, the single best thing we can do for the planet is to keep our stuff in use longer. This simple act of extending the life of our garments through proper care and repair reduces the need to buy more over time—thereby avoiding the CO_2 emissions, waste output, and water usage required to build it." Patagonia partnered with iFixit to publish more than forty free repair guides for Patagonia clothing on its website, in addition to its ongoing operation of the largest garment repair facility in North America and its ongoing training of retail staff to handle simple repairs. One online commentator referred to Marcario's comments as "bizarre declarations" unexpected from a CEO.[22] Beyond being unexpected (a corporate version of why "man bites dog" is newsworthy, rather than the reverse), the extensive, positive visibility Marcario's message generated occurred because Patagonia's corporate character—how it behaves in society, how it expresses itself, and how it engages internally and externally with its vision and values fully integrated into its business strategies—withstands internal and external scrutiny.

The same can be said about the positive visibility often afforded to comments from the CEO of Starbucks, Howard Schultz, and the CEO of Unilever, Paul Polman. If Patagonia's business operations had not credibly aligned with its vision and values, the extensive visibility afforded to Marcario's holiday message would have come in the form of exposés about the hypocrisy of her message or dismissed as a publicity stunt. As the Champion Brand model reflects, the hyper-transparency of today's social landscape means companies cannot showcase a positive initiative and expect to escape scrutiny of the overall way in which it does business.

As more businesses address the twenty-first century reset in what employees and the public now deem as appropriate corporate character, the newsworthiness of holiday messages like Marcario's will wane. Today, however, such messages are still considered surprising.

Negative stereotypes are notoriously sticky, with the residue of skepticism and distrust slow to rub off. Businesses and their leaders likely have plenty of time to pleasantly surprise their publics.

5

THE NEW CORPORATE BRANDING

The relationship between corporate character and corporate brand is reciprocal: Over time, a successful brand comes to stand for or even become synonymous with a corporation, and a corporation guided by its corporate character is positioned to build a resonant and sustainable corporate brand. Today, the corporate brand as an expression of corporate character has become ever more pressing. The growing public expectations for business's role in society and the new social landscape's always-on transparency have combined to drive a raft of issues to the C-suite doorstep, challenging the corporation to act consistently with the values that it has declared are integral to its brand.

As with corporate character, a compelling corporate brand becomes more than its attributes or the sum of its parts. It not only represents how a corporation demonstrates its values and strategies through its actions but also becomes the primary connection between a stakeholder's feelings and perceptions of the organization.

To be sure, there are altogether pragmatic ways to build brand in the context of marketing. This chapter, however, makes the case that the new social landscape has fundamentally reset the business of corporate brand building.

In the new ecosystem of social media, traditional marketing control of the brand message and of the channels to deliver that message has eroded. As a result, understanding the relationship between the corporate brand and corporate character as the foundation of the corporate brand is essential to meeting this new landscape's significant challenges. Today, stakeholders exercise unprecedented scrutiny of the companies behind products, dramatically escalating the importance of the corporate brand and C-suite decisions related to the stakeholder impact on its policies, operations, and governance.

THE DNA OF A CORPORATE BRAND

A corporate brand may be one of the most ubiquitous phenomena of something (a brand) standing for something else (corporate character). The examples in the last chapter could in many ways illustrate how corporate character is made manifest through the corporate brand. Marketing and communications can all too often be seen as concerned primarily with external stakeholders; however, a significant hallmark of the new business environment is that successful brands take on meaning through the fluid interchange between internal and the external stakeholders. As brands have become part of the fabric of popular culture, an understanding of corporate brands requires an understanding of the dynamics embedded in the often-unpredictable context of popular culture.

Many businesses find that their brands have become the single most direct, resonant way they can communicate with their stakeholders. Recent years have seen an emphasis on the consumer, which is all to the good. But aligning a brand exclusively to what a consumer "wants" is not necessarily differentiating, since consumer preferences can be researched by any competitor. Corporate character, however, is unique to each corporation. Through social media's surround-sound scrutiny, today multiple stakeholders can virtually experience the company's corporate character—from the attitudes and actions emanating from the C-suite to interactions with front-line employees—fusing that character with the corporate brand to become an essential differentiator, its DNA.

To a significant extent, "brand" has become so central a term in management because it is the most tangible "intangible" asset. At a product-brand level, you can taste the familiar combination of steamed milk and espresso in a Starbucks latte whether you are at the airport or at a café down the street. And for service brands, the interactions between a passenger and employee at the gate will likely be different if you are flying Singapore Airlines compared with other carriers. Products and services have become part of the now celebrated "experience" economy. While traditional retail stores like Macy's or Staples are closing at a record pace and other retailers like the Limited Stores and Payless have declared bankruptcy, a new category of retail stores is emerging with their physical space optimized for "brand experiences." The new retailers are building an offline community where an online mega disruptor like Amazon is not competing. As the CEO of cosmetic startup Glossier explains, "While the sales are through the roof and defy all odds, what's more interesting are the girls who come once a week because they want to feel the energy in the room," says CEO Emily Weiss. "I can't say that about large beauty retailers."[1]

Besides the alluring aroma of a latte at a Starbucks or the enjoyable experience of visiting New York's Apple store, the customer experience extends beyond the product or service provided or the atmospherics of the store design. It also includes interactions with employees. One can easily imagine how a customer's experience would be affected if the barista serving his or her morning coffee could not share the values of the corporate brand.

As stated by more than one illustrious figure, the phrase "A brand is a promise" captures the relationship between trust and expectations. A product or service brand fulfills its promise by consistently delivering on one's expectations— Ivory soap floats, a FedEx overnight letter arrives not just at its destination but by the next morning—obviously connecting the product or service brand with the organization making the brand promise. The car manufacturer Honda promises reliability. Volvo promises safety. An Aston Martin promises something more exotic. If a product is our main experience with the company, when something goes wrong, it is the company's character that comes into question, damaging both the branded product and the corporate brand.

Volkswagen promised that its diesel cars were environmentally friendly. Covering up a deliberate deceit is a breach of trust directly implicating the corporate brand. Toyota promised, like Honda, reliability and mechanical excellence, which is why its scandal over malfunctioning gas pedals cut to the quick of its brand promise. Honda's airbag malfunction controversy was the fault of an upstream supplier, but it was Honda, not the supplier, that became the focal point of bad news.

A stronger way to state the notion of brand promise is to say "a brand is a contract," a contract between stakeholders on one hand and the brand as the expression or extension of the corporation on the other. The notion of a contract clarifies the company itself as the entity agreeing to a defined relationship, heightening the notion of brand as promise and contextualizing the consequences of breaking that promise as a breach of trust. This explains the "Watergate" axiom that the cover-up is worse than the lapse: Consider Volkswagen's deception related to the environmental regulations on its diesel vehicles and the National Football League's sometimes conflicting acknowledgment of the extent of concussions and chronic traumatic encephalopathy among its players. Professional athletes, it can be argued, if not convincingly, are compensated for taking risks. High school athletes are not.

Organizational theorists significantly advanced the strategic understanding of brands by integrating corporate culture into the study of brands. Mary Jo Hatch and Majken Schultz argue that culture, vision, and image must be aligned to build a brand that will not come undone when gaps emerge between an organization's culture and the perceptions it creates through advertising or management strategy.[2] If strong corporate brands are a function of corporate character, then gaps between culture, vision, and image become crises when the gaps grow too large and visible. Enron's culture of rapacity was exposed hard upon the company's having been celebrated as a new model of visionary strategy for the energy industry. The fusion of corporate culture with the corporate brand mandates that the company's policies, strategies, and governance align with its corporate brand. Gone are the days when corporations could dismiss any criticism of the company as simply an "education" problem that can be corrected by words, not actions.

How does an organization build an enduring corporate brand in the new social context of the twenty-first century? If the issue is an ever-widening gap between eroding trust in and escalating expectations for the role of business in society, how does a corporate brand manage that gap? And how does it do this when hyper-connected internal and external stakeholders can flag those fissures globally with a tweet?

SHIFTING CONTROL OF THE BRAND

Social media has created an alternative universe at a time when the old-line media networks have joined business and government to hit a nadir in public trust. Not to be on Facebook and not to have Twitter is not to exist in this universe. For individuals, not to participate may be considered eccentric. For businesses, an active engagement on social media is required. Engagement in social media is less a matter of virtual reality than having *any* reality, not a matter of being the first on your block but a matter of not living on the block at all.

Beyond the need to engage in social media, the corporate brand implications from this new social media ecosystem are profound. Formerly, brands were built by marketing departments to sell products to external customers. Product brands were built over time by consistently delivering quality. Marketing departments set aside budgets and selected the communication channels through which tested, controlled, and consistent messaging would reach their target customers in known and carefully selected media. In print media, marketing could control which publication would run its advertisements and even the placement location in that publication. In cable or broadcast media, marketing could select programming for its advertising. It could ensure the content of its selected programs aligned with both the brand's attributes and its targeted audience demographics as measured through ratings data.

In short, marketing controlled the branding narrative.

In the new social landscape, traditional marketing control of the corporate brand narrative is an anachronism. To reach a large target audience, social media advertisements are not targeted at specific websites, which would be analogous to selecting specific programming on cable or broadcast channels. Instead, advertisements on social media are typically targeted at specific consumer interests as measured through search or engagement metrics. Problems arise when the targeted consumer interests place advertisements on objectionable websites that are inconsistent with the brand's attributes. As a result, some advertisers have suspended their online ad purchases and Google has developed new tools to give advertisers more control over where their ads appear.[3]

Just as significant, in the social media ecosystem, consumers shape the corporate brand through their experience with the corporation's products and their perceptions of the corporation's business behavior, policies, and practices. A key distinguishing feature of this ecosystem is the ability of consumers to achieve widespread visibility by posting their experiences online. Without this new ecosystem, their alternatives would have been to purchase visibility through advertisements or gain news visibility by convincing gatekeeper journalists to report their stories. Instead, today, the Whole Foods brand can become Whole Paycheck after a series of scandals widely shared online, as discussed in chapter 4. Similarly, a corporate brand's positioning as an employer of choice is perpetually shaped in real-time public postings through websites like Glassdoor, Great Place to Work, Indeed, or Vault.

The new social landscape has shifted control for shaping an organization's corporate brand narrative to its multiple stakeholders whose share of voice has now exponentially increased via social media. This represents a paradigm shift for how corporations advance their brand and thought leadership initiatives. For decades, the process was to advance well tested and controlled messaging through carefully selected communications channels and reliable key opinion leaders. While that process continues, it is no longer sufficient by itself. Instead, in this new landscape, effectively advancing a corporate thought leadership platform or brand narrative means seeking out multiple forming and morphing online communities of interest to find an intersection between those communities' interests and the corporation's desired message. Having found that intersection, a company can then adapt its thought leadership platform or branding message to convey a common interest and engage in a conversation. In the process of exploring the relevant conversations trending online, corporations will sometimes discover unexpected allies and critics shaping the discussions.

Effectively advancing a thought leadership platform or a brand narrative in this new social ecosystem requires an entirely new approach to multi-stakeholder engagement that is quite different from consistently pushing the same, predetermined corporate message through a variety of channels. Failure to recognize this shift and the more expansive and challenging expectations for corporate behavior in the twenty-first century can overlook opportunities for engagement to build stakeholder support for the company and its corporate, product, or service brands or, conversely, erode support by not effectively engaging.

SHARED ADVOCACY

The Champion Brand model discussed in chapter 2 provides a strategic framework navigating this new landscape by mapping key reputational attributes that many corporate brand models have previously recognized: alignment, authenticity, and attachment. But it adds a new attribute crucial to building an enduring corporate brand in this new environment: advocacy.

Like the other Champion Brand elements, advocacy by itself is insufficient. The four elements in the model are not separate but build on each other: Meeting stakeholder expectations by aligning corporate behavior with words is a minimum requirement, without which there would be no basis for authenticity. Authenticity is achieved by an organization doing what it says it will do, reflecting the words and behavior of the entire organization. This includes not only executives' words and actions but also service representatives' online chats with customers or flight attendants' exchanges with passengers during a flight. In the wired world, every personal experience counts and can quickly become a symbol of a corporation's character. Organizations that act authentically and with integrity build trust with stakeholders. Trust alone, however, is insufficient to build an enduring brand without attachment—a personal, emotional connection that builds brand loyalty.

The pinnacle of performance for an enduring champion-brand company in the new business environment is advocacy—not advocacy in the sense of lobbying or lawyering, nor isolated to a for-profit corporation's strategic philanthropy, but advocacy that represents the common interests and values shared by both a for-profit corporation and society. In fact, this definition of advocacy turns the long-followed marketing practice of trying to build brand advocates on its head. Advocacy in this context means being a corporation being *for* something that is directly relevant both to advancing the corporation and addressing a societal need. It represents a high bar: To build a strong and enduring relationship with society, a corporation has a self-interest to champion matters that are important to both itself and society—a shared advocacy.

This does not mean detaching business from its mandate to make a profit and reward its investors. An unprofitable business is not sustainable. Instead, it means finding the "both–and" opportunities discussed in chapter 1. It means fully integrating a corporate vision with supporting strategies, operations, and policies that act in the interest of both an enterprise and society. Just as important, it is the sum of all four Champion Brand levels, not discrete initiatives undertaken as part of cause-based marketing, for example, or disparate corporate social responsibility initiatives. Nor is it isolated to CEO activism when represented by a single executive who is passionate about a discreet cause. Advocacy in this context means a way of doing business as represented not only by a corporation's CEO or executive management, but also reflecting the character of the entire corporation through its words and actions. Shared advocacy demonstrates the reciprocity between a corporate brand and corporate character.

Today, the social media ecosystem, activist nongovernmental organizatons, and the next generation of employees are transforming the concept of a successful corporation: In addition to creating financial value, a successful corporation should conduct its business in a way that also benefits society. A frustrated, restless global public today is seeking solutions to pressing social needs in an era when government and political leaders have become unwilling or less able to serve the public good. As a counterweight to governmental inaction, corporations can enact profitable and socially beneficial operational changes without needing to pass legislation or enact regulation. Depending on their global scale, their impact can be transformational.

TAKING POSITIONS

Reflecting the rising recognition of both the importance of advocacy and the intersection between business and society, stories of corporations taking high-profile positions on social issues have become increasingly common news items, as the public's expectations for and scrutiny of the role of business in society has grown, particularly among millennials. News headlines and social media thoroughly reported on companies like Eli Lilly and Levi Strauss, and even NASCAR, protesting Indiana's Religious Freedom Restoration Act signed by then-governor Mike Pence, threatening to curtail business in the state. The Charlotte Regional Visitors Authority estimates that North Carolina's "bathroom law" banning transgender people from using public bathrooms that do not match the gender they were assigned at birth has cost the state more than $80 million in lost business.[4] Even small businesses in Texas protested state legislators' plans to draft transgender legislation like North Carolina's. The two hundred small business owners in Texas who issued an open letter to state legislators captured the shared interest of business and society in opposing the legislation: "That kind of legislation doesn't just go against our values to be welcoming to everyone, it jeopardizes the businesses we've worked so hard to create, and threatens the jobs and livelihoods of everyday Texans."[5] However, the fact that businesses taking such positions is newsworthy, rather than business as usual, demonstrates that this kind of advocacy is still perceived as far from the norm.

Ironically, however, in the often-polarized world of social media, particularly after the contentious 2016 U.S. presidential election, even corporations who have not engaged by taking a position on timely social issues can quickly find themselves inadvertently caught in an advocacy crossfire of partisan politics. L.L.Bean, which had not endorsed any candidate, found itself the target of an online boycott (referred to with the Twitter hashtag #GrabYourWallet) after an heiress to the Bean fortune became a public advocate of and donor to a pro-Trump political action committee. The L.L.Bean online boycott triggered a tweet from Donald Trump encouraging support for the company, which served only to increase the controversy's visibility.[6] New Balance found its brand similarly caught in the partisan crossfire, with a brand boycott accelerated by a neo-Nazi blogger calling New Balance shoes "the official shoe of white people."[7] The stunning velocity of these boycotts—no matter the inaccurate, confusing, or nuanced facts involved in triggering them—demonstrates that any corporation and corporate brand are now intricately woven into the social fabric of popular culture.

BUSINESS AS A FORCE FOR SOCIAL CHANGE

Apart from partisan politics, the emergence of B Corporation certification shows that shared interests and shared advocacy uniting for-profit businesses and society are not simply a transient business fad. Instead it demonstrates a growing recognition that business is a dominant force with the potential to deliver social changes for the better. B Lab, a nonprofit organization, certifies companies that meet a performance threshold for creating value for both shareholders and nonshareholding stakeholders. Certified companies, also known as B Corps, amend their corporate charter to incorporate those interests into the fiduciary duties of directors and officers. Between 2007, the year B Corporation certification began, and 2017, more than 2,000 corporations in fifty countries had become certified.[8]

The business models of B Corporations like Toms Shoes and Warby Parker consist of selling products in a way that directly benefits society. For Toms, it means applying revenues gained to the distribution of shoes to the poor in developing countries. For Warby Parker, it means deploying its revenues from eyeglass sales to provide eyeglasses to those who cannot afford to buy them. Both examples suggest a market for consumers who want to feel good about a company that integrates its social impact into the core of its business model. Even these altruistic firms, however, are open to critique. Instead of expensive Toms shoes, why not make a donation to a nongovernmental organization? This decision would require diverting the impulse to purchase a pair of shoes to writing a cheque or going online to make a donation to a charitable organization like Oxfam instead, which is probably less likely to get shoes or glasses to people who need them.

In addition to a B Certified Company is a corporate entity called benefit corporation. Both categories are part of a conscious capitalism movement to use for-profit businesses as a force for solving society's most pressing challenges. While a B Certified Corporation can be any type of for-profit legal entity, for example a for-profit law firm, a benefit corporation is a type of corporation authorized by thirty-one states in the United States and the District of Columbia, thereby providing the legal protection of a government recognized legal entity. A benefit corporation's directors and officers are required to consider the impact of their decisions not only on shareholders but also on society and the environment. Patagonia is both a B Corp, first certified by B Lab in 2011, and a benefit corporation as of the first day in 2012 when that status became legally effective for California-based companies.[9] In 2017, DanoneWave, a merger of WhiteWave Foods and Danone's dairy business, became the largest public benefit corporation in the United States, with more than $6 billion in revenue and six thousand employees.[10]

BALANCING THE INTERESTS OF SELF AND SOCIETY

The shared advocacy adopted by these companies is a high bar but one that is directly relevant to restoring trust in terms of what Coca-Cola's chairman and former CEO, Muhtar Kent, calls the transformed consumer landscape, a landscape transformed by information. Beyond B Corporations and benefit corporations, businesses that mitigate stakeholder impact from inherent negatives and advocate interests shared with its key audiences are restoring trust and building their corporate brands. There can be a fine balance between sincere attempts to make a difference and where the business case comes into play.

This can be seen in one of Coca-Cola's more forward-leaning examples of sustainability, the EKOCENTER. These self-contained units, originally constructed from shipping containers, are brought to remote locations in Africa, Asia, and South America that do not have town centers. They provide water purification, electricity, and Internet access, and, while not branded with a logo, they also have Coke for sale. They aim neither to make money or lose money. The EKO-CENTER lies perhaps somewhere between philanthropy and corporate brand building.[11]

EKOCENTERs purify water with "slingshot" technology. Arable water has been a central issue to Coca-Cola, illustrating a clear correspondence between mitigating an inherent negative in a company's business model and finding solutions that are in the interests of both Coca-Cola and society. As Coca-Cola's Greg Koch, senior director of global water stewardship, points out, "Without water you do not have Coke." Water is plainly an essential element in Coca-Cola's supply chain. After running risk assessments on sustainable water around the world, Koch and his team found that a bottling plant consumes more water than ends up inside a bottle of Coke. If a supply of water is being depleted by Coca-Cola, then monetizing water as a commercial product becomes problematic for the company. Sustaining the supply of water is a mutually beneficial advocacy platform Coca-Cola shares with society.

Just as Coca-Cola cannot bottle its beverages without water, neither can it do so without containers. Plastic bottles, however, contribute to waste as well as pollution. Coca-Cola's "PlantBottle" packaging, developed through investment in research and development, is a plastic bottle often used for its bottled-water brand Dasani. The bottle is the first-ever fully recyclable polyethylene terephthalate (PET) plastic bottle and is made partially from plants. Production of the bottles reduces the company's carbon dioxide emissions.[12] It is just one intervention in Coca-Cola's supply chain to mitigate its negative impact but a promising one. Coca-Cola's sustainability report targets 2020 to replenish 100 percent of the water it uses globally, a target it achieved in 2015. It has also committed to expand use of its PlantBottles and extend its potential impact by sharing its PlantBottle technology with Ford, Kraft Heinz, and other large companies. As one manager put it, a water bottle partially made from plants is one thing; extending that to the inside of a car is another. Perhaps one corporation cannot save the world, but consortiums of large multinationals sharing investments in research and development are promising in their potential to have a collective impact.

The societal headwinds facing soda companies related to America's consumption of sugar and the obesity epidemic are significant. As Coca-Cola managers readily admit, being the world's number-one beverage company with soda remaining a central product in a portfolio of more than three thousand products presents challenges. Drawing on its heritage, Coca-Cola has reprised retro-inspired open coolers holding the famous contoured 6.5-ounce bottle, which appeared in 1916 and which Robert Woodruff, president of Coca-Cola from 1923 until 1954, kept as the company's sole product size long after competitors appeared on the scene with larger-sized portions. At present, Coca-Cola managers are quite serious about enjoying Coke in smaller, healthier portions. Eight-ounce plastic bottles and seven-ounce cans are now available, as well as Coke Zero and Green Coke, which address concerns over calorie content and sugar by being made with sugar substitutes.

Recognizing the same headwinds, as part of its "Performance with Purpose" commitment, two-thirds of PepsiCo's beverage portfolio will contain one hundred calories or fewer from added sugar per twelve-ounce serving by 2025. In addition to smaller sizing for carbonated soft drinks, the PepsiCo chairperson and CEO, Indra Nooyi, is addressing the calorie count on many other fronts. "Technology breakthroughs right now are resulting in better-tasting colas, almost as good as full-sugar colas, but with lower calories," she has explained. "So now we are faced with [an] interesting opportunity to step the consumer down to lower sweetness levels." PepsiCo's focus on research and development as part of the solution recognizes that reduced-calorie beverages must still be appealing for consumers to sustain a commercially viable product and healthier choices. "The consumer can't tell the difference, and that is the greatest thing about all of the R&D work, which is now yielding results," says Nooyi.[13]

Nooyi's comments show that she recognizes that producing a healthier product will not have much enduring positive social impact if it does not satisfy the craving of a consuming public, which might opt for several servings of the smaller-sized products. This issue recalls a previous era's efforts to reduce the harm of smoking through cigarettes with lower levels of tar and nicotine. The result was that many smokers adopted compensating behaviors like smoking more cigarettes, smoking them down farther, or inhaling more deeply. The bigger challenge to addressing obesity is to make food products that are both healthy and appealing.

All of this is part of Nooyi's philosophy for conducting business in the twenty-first century in a way that unites and advocates for the shared interests of business and society. She states, "To succeed in today's volatile and changing world, corporations must do three things exceedingly well: focus on delivering strong financial performance, do it in a way that is sustainable over time and be responsive to the needs of society."[14]

SHARED SOLUTIONS

Many corporations who are adjusting their business strategies and operations to the challenges and expectations of the twenty-first century are finding that the problems facing both their businesses and society are so daunting that the solutions must be shared. "The issues we are facing are so big and the targets so challenging that we cannot do it alone so there is a certain humility and recognition that we need to invite other people in," explains the CEO of Unilever, Paul Polman. "When you look at any issue, such as food or water scarcity, it is very clear that no individual institution, government or company can provide the solution." Of particular concern for Polman is the lack of progress from governments. Countries that represent more than half of the globe's domestic gross product are stymied by constantly changing political leadership consisting of people who are increasingly unwilling to lead or act decisively when dealing with an increasingly impatient, frustrated public. Business, says Polman, must step in to lead. "Business," Polman declares, "is now in the driving seat on many of the initiatives such as the moratorium on illegal deforestation."[15]

Addressing deforestation by sourcing sustainable palm oil is exhibit A for illustrating the need to advocate shared solutions that are bigger than any single business, government, nongovernmental organization, or local supplier can provide. Palm oil is a staple ingredient of vegetable oil found in thousands of consumer products. It is extracted from the fruit pulp of the oil palm, a high-yielding plant that provides an economic livelihood for millions of farmers in Indonesia and Malaysia and is increasingly farmed in Africa and Latin America. An important ingredient for Unilever's margarine, ice cream, soap, and shampoos, the demand for palm oil continues to grow. Western consumer-goods companies, however, account for only 20 percent of global palm oil sales. The volume from local traders in emerging markets like China account for the balance.

The enormous global demand for palm oil has become a major catalyst for clearing existing forests—which are critical to preserving biodiversity and ecosystems that yield watershed protection and fertile soil and for mitigating climate change—accounting for over half of all land conversion.

In 2009, Unilever committed to a long-term goal of sourcing 100 percent of its palm oil sustainably and has more broadly committed to source 100 percent of its agricultural raw materials sustainably by 2020. But given the global demand for palm oil, the problem is bigger than Unilever's unilateral actions can address. In addition to requiring its direct and third-party suppliers to agree to its sustainable palm oil sourcing policy, Unilever is leveraging its scale to influence the rest of the industry, working with peer companies, nongovernmental organizations, and other multi-stakeholder groups globally. In 2016, Unilever brought forward its target for purchasing 100 percent physically certified palm oil from 2020 to 2019.[16]

Unilever's focus on finding shared solutions even extends to changing its customers' behaviors. The company found that 68 percent of the greenhouse gas emissions from the carbon footprint of two thousand of its products occurred once the products were downstream in the hands of customers, primarily from heating water; for example, heating water for tea, washing one's hands with soap, and washing one's hair with shampoo. One solution to reducing the downstream carbon footprint from consumers using its existing products is to change consumer habits, like encouraging shorter showers. Another is to invest research and development in profitable new products specifically designed to consume fewer natural resources when used. For example, Unilever's dry shampoos work when combed through the hair, not as a total replacement for a traditional hot-water shampoo but as a water-saving, convenient alternative in between shampoos. As a result, the company can sell a new, profitable product and also benefit society.[17] However, as a reminder that traditional business fundamentals still matter, dry shampoo also has its critics, with social media stories gaining traction in some networks that dry shampoo can cause hair loss and scalp injuries. Many experts attribute such reactions to using the product as a full substitute for traditional shampoos rather than as a between-shampoo alternative. Unilever nonetheless addressed the dispute for its Suave brand with a $10 million class action settlement.[18] Despite that criticism, sales of Unilever's dry shampoos are growing with global revenue expanding by 14 percent in 2016 and achieving a 38 percent market share for the dry shampoo category in the United States.[19]

In another example, women in drought-affected South Africa using Unilever's new Sunlight handwashing powder with foam-reducing technology have been able to halve the number of rinses required, saving them time when hand washing laundry and saving water. Products like these are among Unilever's Sustainable Living brands which are the company's leading products that have purpose and sustainability at their core. In 2016, its Sustainable Living brands grew more than 50 percent faster than the rest of its business and delivered more than 60 percent of Unilever's overall growth.[20]

GlobeScan, a public opinion consultancy, named Unilever as the global leader in sustainability for the sixth consecutive year in 2016, a record no other company has maintained in the nineteen-year history of the survey.[21] While this result is extremely laudable, it might be tempting to view Unilever's remarkable corporate brand ranking exclusively as a function of its all-in embrace of sustainability. However, Unilever's way of doing business today is firmly rooted in its cultural history, including a period of time well before sustainability became a global imperative.

From the start, William Lever, who along with his brother, James, founded Lever Brothers, which would become Unilever, viewed business holistically. Unilever built the town of Port Sunlight to provide decent housing for employees and provided education, health care, and good wages for its employees at palm oil plantations in the Congo. Further, the company marketed products like Lifebuoy soap for the health benefits of clean hands at a time when disease and malnutrition were widespread in Britain.

When Paul Polman became CEO in 2009, he prioritized long-term results, reducing shares held by hedge funds from 15 percent to 5 percent in three years by attracting long-term investment funds to buy the company's stock. Beyond its financial backing and sustainable product and sourcing strategies, the engagement score result for Unilever's more than 170,000 employees—a measure of how inclined employees are to feel and speak positively about their workplace—in a worldwide Gallup poll was an astounding 80 percent; the average corporate engagement score was just 13 percent.[22] Unilever's corporate brand and corporate character, like the other positive examples discussed in this chapter, are reciprocal and mutually supportive, and its vision, strategies, and policies not only align, but also drive authenticity, attachment, and ultimately shared advocacy.

If strengthening stakeholder engagement to the level of shared advocacy builds an enduring brand, falling short of a claimed shared advocacy may expose an organization to significant business risks. After promising cars that were more environmentally friendly, Volkswagen is now settling its emissions scandal at a cost of nearly $20 billion and climbing. The true costs will go much further as the German automaker cuts thousands of jobs to reduce costs and investigations continue.[23]

One might feel compelled to argue that scandals of this type have always existed, that there is nothing new here. This is true enough, but because of the Internet and social media, news travels farther and exponentially faster than ever before, and it would be naïve to think that the pace at which news travels will remain the same in the future. Additionally, news stories remain on the Internet as a constant reminder of failed trust. Like diamonds, the Internet is forever.

Strategically, building and stewarding an enduring corporate brand in this new era is more expansive and challenging than just a decade ago when marketing still largely controlled the brand narrative. At the leading edge of executives who have recognized the need for a strategic reset in the relationship between business and society is the not-for-profit B Team established in 2013 by British entrepreneur Sir Richard Branson and former Puma CEO Jochen Zeitz. The B Team represents a "Plan B" for a new kind of capitalism more oriented to socially responsible long-term results.[24] The new collective has brought together a small group of globally influential leaders drawn from businesses, nongovernmental organizations, and government to drive transformational change in the business sector. Plan B advocates a new model for capitalism itself that expands corporate accountability to include responsibility for not only financial results but also for the corporation's negative and positive contributions to the economy, environment, and society.[25] The B Team's launch statement claims as its goal to deliver "a new way of doing business that prioritises [sic] people and planet alongside of profit—a 'Plan B' for business the world over." At the global enterprise level, initiatives like the B Team have largely been catalyzed by the need to recruit the next-generation workforce who have high expectations for business and who see the urgent need posed by a growing global population whose demand for vital resources like food and water is projected to exceed the supply. It is also a logical sequel to the hard lessons learned from the freewheeling economic model in the financial sector that crashed in 2008.

SMALL AND MEDIUM-SIZED ENTERPRISES

This reconfigured approach to business, however, is not limited to large, multinational corporations. As N. Craig Smith, INSEAD Chair in Ethics and Social Responsibility, points out, small and medium-sized enterprises (SMEs), those with up to 1,000 employees, also have intrinsic and business case motivations for strategies benefitting both their business and society. "SME's are generally managed by their owners, who are often their founders. This can lead to profound differences in commitment to corporate purpose. Few successful entrepreneurs start businesses solely with the intent of making money. This was true of William Lever when he founded the business that became Unilever—selling soap saved lives," explains Smith. In addition to starting a business motivated by a purpose, personal relationships with employees, suppliers and local communities are often key to SMEs' success, engendering supportive operating strategies. Finally, according to Smith, SMEs that become part of a large enterprise's supply chain increasingly participate in that enterprise's value chain of sustainability practices, metrics, and performance.[26] In some cases, giant multinationals acquire relatively smaller enterprises attracted by their natural, worker-friendly, socially responsible, and profitable businesses. Colgate Palmolive acquired Tom's of Maine's natural ingredient consumer products business for $100 million; Clorox Company purchased Burt's Bees with its all-natural personal care products for $913 million; and Unilever acquired Ben and Jerry's Homemade—whose mission statement promises products "incorporating wholesome, natural ingredients and promoting business practices that respect the Earth and the Environment"—for $326 million.[27]

As in any acquisition, whether the shared advocacy and purpose of these companies survive the merger often depends on a shared culture. In 2011 when Danone, a global $25 billion multinational food corporation, acquired start-up Happy Family Brands, a small B Certified Corporation, the large-scale multinational and small business found themselves united in a common purpose. "Danone," says Lorna Davis, CEO of DanoneWave and Danone's Chief Manifesto Catalyst, "has a mission to bring health through food to as many people as possible" which includes a business stream specifically focused on early-life nutrition. Happy Family Brands founder and CEO Shazi Visram launched her company, originally named Happy Baby, "to kind of change the world with organic baby food," she explains. Visram's Happy Family Brands became a subsidiary of Group Danone because its fast growth was threatening its long-term sustainability as a business. "We were growing so fast, we needed a partner," she says.[28]

Beyond their shared purpose, the two companies also had mutual needs coming from opposite ends of the corporate size spectrum. As Visram explains, "Those of us who are in smaller B Corps who are fighting the good fight every day . . . I could fight the rest of my life to make the impact Lorna's been able to make with her wherewithal in the two years that I have known her." For multinational Danone, explains Davis, "One of the things we're inspired by with the whole B Corporation movement is that we believe that the people you spend your time with are people you become like. . . . Just as a B Corp is needing to scale with integrity, we're needing to move and change and transform with integrity too."[29] As a member of B Lab's Multinationals and Public Market Advisory Council, Danone is helping to bridge the barriers to B Corp Certification faced by most private and publicly listed multinationals.[30]

In contrast to the Happy Family Brands scenario for a smaller company pursuing profit with purpose, Chobani founder and CEO Hamdi Ulukaya rejected multiple offers from potential investors taking a different path for his upstate New York startup yogurt company. In a decade, he grew Chobani from 5 to 2,000 employees with $1 billion in annual sales. Ulukaya financed his company's growth through bank loans and reinvested profits. His rationale for rejecting offers from private equity firms reinforces Professor Smith's observations on entrepreneurs' intrinsic and business motivations. In his *Harvard Business Review* article, CEO Ulukaya explained, "as soon as I took money from investors, the clock would start ticking. Private equity investors want to cash out in five to seven years—they would probably push us to sell Chobani to a big food company. I've seen small food companies go that route, and inevitably lose their souls. I care about the integrity of our product—I want to be delicious, nutritious and accessible to everyone." He decided to stop returning prospective investors' calls.[31]

A sole owner of the company, Ulukaya decided to share a portion of his company with employees in 2016 by giving them what he called "Chobani Shares." He told employees to think of the shares as a grant to expand the company even more. In the future, in the event of Chobani becoming publicly traded or being sold, employees can convert their Chobani Shares, collectively worth up to 10 percent of the company, to stock or cash. "We used to work together; now we are partners. . . . We built something; now we are sharing it," he told employees, one-third of whom are refugees. In addition, Ulukaya donates 10 percent of Chobani profits to charity.[32]

Whether for large or small businesses, in today's landscape, the new corporate brand accrues in value based on the quality of a corporation's stakeholder relationships, with the stakeholders themselves driving the corporate brand narrative: Customers shape a brand through their experience with it, employees through their relationships with both peers and management, nongovernmental organizations through their public comments on the organization's behavior, and so on.

As the ability to shape the organization's corporate brand continues to shift to its stakeholders, a successful, enduring business is no longer exclusively defined by profitably delivering a product or service. It is also defined by its footprint in society as judged by its web-enabled stakeholders who are perpetually auditing its actions. Mitigating its inherent negatives has become a minimum requirement, table stakes for doing business. Today, sustainable and enduring corporate brands must profitably deliver products and services in a way that also benefits society, addressing the intersection of where its operations, scale, and capabilities can also positively transform unmet social needs.

6

REPUTATION LOST AND FOUND

A s was said of Macbeth's predecessor, "Nothing in his life became him like the leaving it." To paraphrase, nothing quite illuminates reputation as much as losing it. If an "intangible asset," reputation, once lost, has altogether tangible results: loss of market share, a decline in share price; damage to a brand, and, not least, loss of trust.

Traditionally, reputation made "business sense" as a general hedge against risk that might escalate to crisis, scandal, or bad news. Dell, for example, for many years was a *Fortune* "most admired company" based largely on trust in the management of Michael Dell. When the company was public, Dell could miss a quarterly earnings projection with less effect on share price than a "generic" brand like Compaq. The market would give it a break. When United Technologies struggled in the 1990s, analysts running break-up models on the conglomerate were in part influenced by trust in Steve Page, who had been CFO at Black and Decker before joining United Technologies. Even investment bankers who remain resistant to the idea of intangible assets nevertheless include those assets in their calculation of share price and valuation.

The instant transparency of the new social landscape, however, has collapsed the effectiveness of these previous hedges against risk and shortened the ramp time for a developing crisis. Recognizing that a crisis, like the weather, is something that people always talk about but never seem to stop, this chapter deals with reputations lost and found in today's dramatically changed environment for conducting business.

CROWDSOURCED RATINGS AND RANKINGS

Since reputation is, simply stated, what other people say about you, not what you say about yourself, it lends itself to public opinion tracking and ratings, with reputation scoring systems gaining increased visibility in the optimistic 1990s after the 1990–1991 recession began to recede and before the dot-com bubble burst. While companies were unsure of this intangible asset, the common wisdom was that you could not let competitors have an advantage in this arena. Charles Fombrun's widely recognized "reputation quotient" staked out the managerial and practitioner territory. Fombrun based his reputation rating system on a set of categories tied to weighted algorithms: emotional appeal, products and services, workplace environment, financial performance, vision and leadership, and social responsibility. Soon, the Harris Poll began offering highly publicized reputation quotient rankings, and *Fortune* expanded its published yearly rankings of most admired companies to include various dimensions, including best managed, best to work for, and best for the environment. Like college rankings in *U.S. News and World Report*, corporate reputation rankings proliferated to other well-known publications that recognized the sales promotion value of these rankings and dedicated resources to managing the polls.

Many of these rankings offer a point-in-time snapshot of reputation, which has value comparable to a mile marker on a map, providing a general indication of being on or off course by telling you where you are on a certain date compared with other companies. Unless designed with statistical tools, such as regression analysis, to understand relationships among variables, a reputation snapshot cannot reliably inform a path forward to where you want to go, particularly important to companies today charting strategies when the rules of engagement between business and society have changed so dramatically.

A distinctly new consequence of the new social landscape has been the democratization of ratings, fundamentally collapsing the barriers to entry (to use a strategic marketing concept) for creating scorekeeping systems. Rather than reputation evolving predominantly through carefully managed long-term marketing campaigns or reputation scoring confined to proprietary algorithms, today online word-of-mouth crowdsourcing scores have proliferated to rate virtually everything as it happens. Ratings on a social media platform like Yelp influence restaurant selection at the moment reservations are made. Customer reviews posted on mega sites like Amazon provide real-time ratings not only of a product but also commentary on the corporation behind it, including the responsiveness of a company's customer service employees and its track record of honoring warranties.

In the high expectations–low trust context in which businesses now operate, word of mouth from employees, friends, or other unofficial sources has gained preference, magnifying the reputational impact of personal assessments and crowdsourced scoring on social media. The perpetually updated scoring of products and services shapes both the public's expectations and companies' reputations, often at the moment when purchase decisions are being made, potentially creating a business impact. A UCLA study, for example, credited online reviews for lessening the revenue advantage some branded hotel chains like La Quinta or Super 8 have had over independent hotels. While branded chains still retain the revenue lead, independent hotels have narrowed the margin. After controlling for other factors, the study attributed online reviews as a major factor.[1] In addition to now-instant scoring systems, instant boycotts resulting from campaigns like #GrabYourWallet in the hyper-partisan environment following the 2016 U.S. presidential election can gain momentum in a matter of minutes. And tweets from President Trump can put a company in the crossfire of boycotters and supporters, as was the case with Nordstrom's decision to stop carrying the Ivanka Trump brand.

Given the unprecedented, instant transparency fundamental to conducting business in the twenty-first century, reputation can be lost in record time. This new context places a premium on proactively anticipating the impact of a business's actions through the lens of increasingly diverse stakeholders. In some cases, as we argued in chapter 3, proactively anticipating inherent negatives embedded in a company's business model—that is, negative stakeholder impacts that multiply as the business expands—can not only mitigate risk but may also reveal opportunities for new business strategies. Waste Management, for example, changed its business model from one dependent on its customers generating an increasing volume of waste, an obvious inherent negative, to one in which they converted their knowledge of waste management into waste reduction, a new business strategy central to their growth. In addition to a strategic pivot like Waste Management's, however, the trust-expectations gap in today's always-on, web-empowered social landscape requires an outside-in, diverse stakeholder perspective as an ongoing way of doing business.

That 360-degree anticipation, however, is not easy. As we have acknowledged, many things obstruct the corporate view through the windshield. Rather than sudden events like product tampering, according to the Institute for Crisis Management's annual reviews, crises from smoldering issues within management's control are more common, but often not detected before they erupt. Wells Fargo's fraudulent banking account scandal, for example, smoldered within the company for years without substantive management intervention until it spiraled into a crisis due to a *Los Angeles Times* investigative report published in 2013. A Wells Fargo Board of Directors' investigative report publicly released in 2017 criticized management's failure to act, despite mounting internal evidence of the scandal. While some media called the board report "scathing," others called it a "whitewash" for failing to hold the board itself accountable.[2] Crises have continued to erupt at such a pace that crisis management has reached pop culture status, with a popular television show like *Scandal* starring a political crisis manager.

CASE STUDIES IN REPUTATIONS LOST AND FOUND

Because a full-blown crisis places a company's communications function on the front line, crisis management is often viewed as a functional responsibility and specialized expertise owned by the company's chief communications officer (CCO). As most CCOs who have managed major crises will counsel, however, strategically navigating a sustainable path forward in a crisis is a mandate for the larger executive management team. As a predicate for finding the right messaging, the first order of business in recovering from a crisis-damaged reputation is making good business decisions, not wordsmithing. Selecting business policies to change and constructive actions to take is crucial to building the foundation for a solution and potentially a common ground with the stakeholders impacted. Those business decisions and actions become the content of effective communications and engagement. Reputations are rebuilt on actions effectively implemented and communicated that directly address the breach of trust caused by the crisis. Imagining, inventing, debating, and deciding on those actions, not simply searching for effective messaging, is the first priority for a management team with a diverse 360-degree stakeholder perspective on the issue at hand. Particularly in this new landscape, and given that millennials have likely not yet made it to the

C-suite, understanding the view of millennials on potential constructive actions has become critical for the crisis management team, given the degree of activism among this generation. The CEO of Facebook, Mark Zuckerberg, quickly found that out after initially dismissing Facebook's responsibility to act on the issue of fake news, a view that required a course correction.

An in-depth look at how Aetna and Dow Corning lost and rebuilt their reputations following bet-the-company crises is instructive, with lessons learned that are especially relevant in today's new social landscape. The direct observations of central players in both crises, with their insights seasoned by the passage of time, provide a unique insight into the management strategies and decisions central to recovering the companies' reputations. The Aetna profile is based on this book's authors' extensive interviews with Aetna's executive management team who addressed the crisis, including Roger Bolton, who was, at the time of the crisis, Aetna's CCO and is now president of the Arthur W. Page Society.[3] The Dow Corning profile is based on coauthor Barie Carmichael's direct role as Dow Corning's CCO and member of the company's executive management team, as well as this book's authors' decade-long collaboration as part of the University of Virginia's Darden Graduate School of Business Batten Fellows Program, which included developing the concept of inherent negatives and the oppositional crisis model for crisis management.[4]

Both cases occurred during what was then still emerging as the new social landscape for business, with issues building in the 1990s and ultimately being resolved in 2003 and 2004. Rather than social media acting as the crises' accelerant, high-profile litigation led by product-liability lawyers—flush from collecting an estimated $10 billion to $30 billion from tobacco litigation—drove both crises through class actions, creating widespread and years-long visibility. What is critical, however, is that, in both cases, the foundation for resolving the crises and restoring reputation rested on key business strategies and actions to mitigate stakeholder impact from business practices inherent in each company's business model, decisions that were fundamental regardless of whether the catalyst was a lawsuit or a social media storm. Understanding how each company determined the constructive actions needed to resolve its crisis is the critical point.

THE LEAD VILLAIN IN MANAGED CARE

In 1990, Aetna was ranked by *Fortune* as the nation's fifth most admired financial services company. But by the spring of 2003, Aetna had been cast in news reports as the lead villain in managed-care insurance, portrayed as inflicting onerous policies on patients and physicians that put profit above the well-being of customers. In 1996, the nearly 150-year-old company had divested its property-and-casualty business to focus on health care and retirement services, a strategic pivot following a sustained track record as a multiline insurer that had navigated crises like the San Francisco earthquake in 1906 and the Great Depression. By 1999, through acquisitions and organic growth, Aetna had become the largest U.S. provider of health benefits, with twenty-one million subscribers.

Bigger, however, was not necessarily better as fundamental changes emerging in the 1990s reconfigured the business model for delivering health care. Health maintenance organizations (HMOs) had initially promised to deliver better health care through cost-effective best practices that would reduce spiraling health care costs by combining the discipline of quality process management with computerized claims processing: a win–win for business and stakeholders. As the HMO business model continued to grow, however, the negative impacts on stakeholders inherent in the business model became increasingly visible. Physicians and patient stakeholders perceived insurers as intervening in the doctor–patient relationship. Physicians felt insurers were second-guessing their medical judgment, adding significant administrative costs to their medical practice, and potentially endangering their patients' health by restricting what they saw as appropriate care. Patients felt insurers were preventing access to needed treatments, and patients without employer-based insurance found themselves excluded from in-network medical care discounts, pricing them out of the market.

For Aetna, being the biggest simply multiplied the collective negative impact of its policies and procedures, making them first among eight insurers targeted for class action, with their stock dropping 18 percent in one day when the news first leaked of the impending class action. "All of these massive lawsuits came down to fundamental business practices that were symptomatic of aspects of the business model that angered physicians," explained Robert Stillman, Aetna's corporate counsel at the time.

BREAKING OUT OF THE CORPORATE BUBBLE

By 2000, Aetna recognized the crisis needed more than tweaks in its legal or communications tactics, naming John Rowe, MD, as its new CEO and president. An esteemed gerontologist and the former CEO of Mt. Sinai Health Systems in New York City, Rowe brought a stakeholder's perspective to Aetna's situation, which he estimated in 2001 was losing about $1 million a day. Rowe understood that what Aetna needed was more than re-engineered operations for better efficiency and cost reduction, although operational excellence was critical to enabling Aetna's restored reputation. Instead, Aetna needed to change many of its counterproductive processes and business practices, like the pre-certification requirement for a treatment or procedure. "In some cases," Rowe explained, "that requirement made sense. But in other cases, like requiring pre-certification before performing a cesarean section, it was silly since the procedure would not have been denied anyway." As the industry leader, if Aetna left inherently flawed processes unchallenged, the damage would be replicated thousands of times given the volume of Aetna's claims.

Rowe's position as a physician allowed him to break out of the corporate bubble, ask uncomfortable questions, and see the inherent negatives in Aetna's business model. Even more importantly, he saw the potential to convert the inherent negatives in its managed-care business model into inherent strengths in a transformed business model that benefited both business and society, an early example of a shared value. He saw the insurer's ability to prove the business case for quality care, not simply cost-effective care, through the smarter use of information to yield better medical outcomes. "The value-add of a health plan is more than negotiating and paying claims," Rowe explained. "The information we have about a member can improve the health of patients and can help doctors and patients decide on treatments and options."

Early on, it became clear to Rowe that the class action lawsuit was an impediment to his ability to get doctors on board with his proposed changes to Aetna's policies, so he decided to break from his industry competitors, who were all determined to fight the class action lawsuit in court. Aetna's class action settlement and the restoration of its reputation would be focused on changes in its future business practices that were consistent with its strategy of transforming its managed-care business model. The settlement both advanced Rowe's strategic vision for Aetna and addressed physicians' underlying concerns in ways beyond what a monetary settlement alone could have done.

"THE COUNTRY'S MOST PHYSICIAN-FRIENDLY INSURER"

Institutionalizing new policies and constructive actions, the settlement created a new medical foundation focused on enhancing physicians' ability to provide patients with quality health care, including initiatives to prevent childhood obesity and improve end-of-life care. In language approved by the American Medical Association (AMA), the settlement explicitly gave more weight in Aetna's policies to physicians' clinical judgment as a factor in approved treatments and applied generally accepted medical standards in determining medical necessity. The settlement also established a national advisory committee of practicing physicians to provide ongoing counsel to Aetna and to institutionalize cooperative processes between physicians and Aetna to improve revised managed-care practices. Finally, Aetna would implement information systems that would dramatically increase its openness and transparency with physicians, enabling them to understand their options in advance of treatment, reduce their administrative overhead, and speed up payments.

In all, the settlement totaled $170 million, resulting in an after-tax charge net of insurance of $75 million. Between 2001 and 2006, Aetna transformed itself from a company losing $1 million per day to a company earning $1.9 billion. As *Businessweek*'s Jessi Hempel and Diane Brady summarized in their January 4, 2006, article, "The once notoriously stingy and fiercely unpopular company is now cast as the country's most physician-friendly insurer." Aetna's stock price appreciation between April 11, 2001, and October 24, 2007, was 671 percent. Just as important, by 2009, 84 percent of Aetna's employees said they were proud to work for Aetna, with 87 percent confirming they practiced the "Aetna Way": a summary of the vision, values, and operational strategies that formed the basis for the company's transformation. Those results nearly doubled the company's ratings at the height of the crisis in 2002.[5]

While Rowe clearly led the transformation that brought Aetna back from the edge of the cliff, the diverse, multifunctional management team he put in place architected and implemented the constructive actions and policy revisions that drove the change. That team included, among others, newly recruited executives as well as top legal and communications executives who combined their institutional knowledge with an outside-in understanding of the pressing need for change.[6]

Further, Rowe personally engaged with disaffected stakeholders to understand the changes needed for a new strategic direction. "The Saturday before I started with Aetna," Rowe recalled, "I was invited by the American Medical Association to meet with its board. The first thing I said was that I had been a long-term, dues-paying AMA member. That differentiated Aetna for them." The physician class action, however, became a roadblock to a sustained dialogue with doctors, as Rowe discovered when, prior to commencing settlement discussions, physicians cancelled his meeting with the Connecticut State Medical Society. It became clear that as long as the class action remained in place, progress on Aetna's new strategic redirection enabled through meaningful dialogue with physician stakeholders would be blocked. Settlement discussions needed to be focused on future business practices that would provide a framework to architect a common-ground solution. "The overall settlement involved a mixture of new things not already done, some things that had already been changed, some things Aetna knew it had to do, and some things Aetna did not want to do, but had to do anyway," recalls William Popik, who was Aetna's chief medical officer from 2001 until 2005.[7]

FINDING COMMON GROUND

In any crisis, particularly an oppositional crisis with organized groups contesting polarized positions, the debate can continue with no end in sight, attracting extended media interest that accelerates the controversy, since high-profile disputes drive media organizations' revenues, whether through clicks, viewers, or subscribers. In fact, the new social landscape has increased the likelihood of disruptive oppositional crises. To give one example, the 2016–2017 fake news controversy involving Google or a social media giant like Facebook demonstrates that the "stickiness," visibility, and attractiveness of oppositional crises are just as relevant now as they were during the Aetna crisis, which occurred just at the cusp of this new era. In an oppositional crisis, businesses that get baited into prioritizing "winning" the debate by defeating their critics will only ensure the debate continues. That mindset puts them on the defensive, responding to critics who then ultimately control the narrative. The media— social media, establishment media, mainstream media, alternative media—welcome that approach. Controversy is not only urgent and interesting. It drives media revenue.

A key lesson from Aetna's crisis management strategy, however, is that the company did not seek to win the debate, but to end it through a business strategy based on finding common ground. Rather than focusing on combating its critics and putting itself on the defensive, Aetna pursued common-ground solutions through a changed heath care model that transformed the company's narrative from defense to offense: Aetna could advocate what it was for, not what it was against. To apply the Champion Brand strategic framework to Aetna's crisis management, the company not only *realigned* its operations to correct inherent negatives and meet stakeholder expectations, it also built operational excellence to *authentically* meet those expectations, which grew stakeholder *attachment*, as Aetna became an *advocate* for something bigger than its own interests: a more effective health care system benefiting both business and society. Aetna's statement of "Why We Exist" captures all of these dimensions, defining the company's business through the lens of its stakeholders:

> Aetna is dedicated to helping people achieve health and financial security by providing easy access to safe, cost-effective, high-quality health care and protecting their finances against health-related risks.
>
> Building on our 150-year heritage, Aetna will be a leader, cooperating with doctors and hospitals, employers, patients, public officials and others to build a stronger, more effective health care system.[8]

Although the context of Dow Corning's reputation restoration differs in important ways from Aetna's, the key factors at play following its breast implant crisis have important and instructive parallels with Aetna. And, as with Aetna, the lessons learned from an in-depth, behind-the-scenes understanding of those key factors—playing out as the

power of the Internet and social media was just emerging—
have become even more critical to restoring reputation in
today's new social landscape. Unlike Aetna, Dow Corning
was a privately held company, jointly owned by the Dow
Chemical Company and Corning Incorporated since its
founding on a handshake in 1943. While many confused Dow
Corning with Dow Chemical, the company was a completely
separate legal entity, not a subsidiary, focused on developing
silicon-based materials ranging from the ultra-pure silicon
used in integrated circuits to a vast array of synthetic silicone polymers. As a privately held materials company, Dow
Corning was not consumer facing like Aetna, nor did it have
public stockholders. While the impact of the crisis on Dow
Chemical's and Corning's market value was clearly an issue,
Dow Corning's owners consistently took a long-term strategic view on how the crisis was managed.

Perhaps the most dramatic difference between Aetna's
and Dow Corning's crises was the materiality of the products on which the crises were focused. Aetna's crisis was
focused on the core products of the company that directly
affected its twenty-one million subscribers and their physicians. Dow Corning's crisis was focused on the company's
silicone breast implant products, which never represented
more than 1 percent of its business. The insularity of being
a privately held, predominantly business-to-business company combined with the assumed limited business impact of
breast implants left the company unprepared for a tsunami
of public outrage when the trial bar invested its tobacco and
asbestos winnings into their next mass litigation target.

BEFORE AND AFTER

The most instructive insights from Dow Corning's breast implant crisis can be seen in the dramatic before-and-after dynamics of the issue. The concern centered on whether silicone gel–filled implants caused systemic disease ranging from defined diseases like scleroderma to a less defined constellation of auto-immune symptoms.[9]

The crisis exploded on the scene in the early 1990s with pretrial and verdict publicity in a high-visibility breast implant lawsuit alleging implants caused the plaintiff to contract scleroderma. A record $7.43 million judgment against Dow Corning catapulted the formerly low-profile company into the lead story in a then-emerging 24/7 global news cycle. At the same time, the Food and Drug Administration's (FDA's) new commissioner, David Kessler, had designated breast implants as the first class III medical device to undergo FDA approval since the FDA had been granted authority to regulate medical devices in 1976. Leaked trial evidence from the plaintiffs' attorneys led Kessler to request a moratorium on the sale and implantation of breast implants until further review of the research was conducted, not only escalating and lengthening the media attention but dramatically ramping up the mass filings of lawsuits. Following Kessler's announcement of the moratorium, Dow Corning permanently withdrew from the breast implant market, but as the pioneer of breast implants, the company continued to star as the lead villain in the controversy. By December 1994, the 131 individual lawsuits filed in 1991 had exploded to just under 20,000.[10]

In 1995, however, the trajectory of the issue began to change dramatically. Articles and editorials supporting Dow Corning's position on the safety of breast implants appeared in agenda-setting media including *Fortune*, the *New York Times*, the *Wall Street Journal*, and the *Washington Post*. Then, *60 Minutes* and PBS's investigative *Frontline* aired supportive features explaining the lack of connection between silicone breast implants and auto-immune disease, with extensive interviews with the *New England Journal of Medicine* editor-in-chief, Marcia Angell, and then dean of the Ohio State University College of Medicine, Bernadine Healy.

What changed?

It was not a matter of Dow Corning suddenly adopting more proactive communications strategies, as some analyses of the breast implant crisis case had surmised. Instead, the change was enabled through a new management approach to the crisis through critical strategic business decisions and constructive actions first initiated in 1992, with the results from those decisions and actions slowly emerging in 1995.

AN OUTSIDE-IN PERSPECTIVE

Dow Corning's high-visibility crisis reached a breaking point in 1992, which led to the appointment of a new CEO, Keith McKennon, a Dow Chemical executive with extensive experience in managing high-visibility issues. McKennon brought an intuitive outside-in understanding of the various stakeholder perspectives on the breast implant issue, ranging from those of employees, customers, and local communities to breast implant patients themselves. A survivor of non-Hodgkin's lymphoma, McKennon immediately understood that Dow Corning's first obligation in managing the issue was not to Dow Corning's physician customers but to breast implant patients, many of whom had opted for the implants as they recovered from a mastectomy due to breast cancer. Comparable to Aetna's CEO John Rowe first meeting with the AMA, one of the first things McKennon would disclose when meeting with cancer survivors who had received breast implants was his own experience with cancer. Prior to joining Dow Corning, he also had taken several law school courses so he could both anticipate and intuitively understand the often-opaque world of legal procedures in mass torts. Through both his disposition and personal experience, McKennon brought a fresh stakeholder perspective to the issue.

One of McKennon's first actions was to establish a multi-functional executive issue-management team composed of both new recruits and incumbent executives from diverse backgrounds: the global medical materials business unit leader, the chief counsel, a key toxicologist, the global communications leader, and an expert epidemiologist to name a few. He also elevated global communications to report directly to the executive office, putting that function at the C-suite level. The team met daily, sometimes all day, with some members divesting global operational responsibilities to a second chair within their functional group to devote their full time to managing the issue. McKennon would routinely ask the executive crisis management team the same questions the company's critics had proffered, questions he declared legitimate concerns deserving a candid assessment. Previously, those questions had been smugly dismissed internally as unsubstantiated bogus accusations from the plaintiffs' attorneys. McKennon's questions broke through the corporate bubble. He modeled asking the uncomfortable questions that needed to be answered as a predicate to determining the key decisions and actions the team would take.

A PLATFORM OF CONSTRUCTIVE ACTIONS

Ultimately, the team made critical changes to the company's business strategies and policies as a threshold step to rebuild Dow Corning's reputation. In addition to permanently withdrawing from the breast implant business, Dow Corning implemented three key constructive actions to address the crisis, which McKennon announced in 1992 at a standing room–only press conference in the Washington, DC, press club: (1) The company would fund $10 million of additional research to address the remaining questions about the safety of breast implants, expanding on the existing thirty years of research already conducted and publicly released; (2) Dow Corning would institute a policy such that, before any public health study was initiated, the researchers would commit to the results being published in peer-reviewed medical journals, ensuring public access to what would normally have been proprietary product research; and (3) Dow Corning would institute a fund to provide up to $5,000 to any woman with Dow Corning breast implants who wanted to have them removed but lacked the financial means to do so.

Taken together, those constructive actions transformed Dow Corning from a combative, defensive posture honed from battling plaintiffs' attorneys into an advocate for getting women the information they needed to make an informed decision about their implants, regardless of whether they intended to or had already filed a lawsuit against the company. They would have access to additional peer reviewed research about the products and, if they needed it, they had financial assistance to have their Dow Corning implants removed. Dow Corning was now positioned as *for* an informed choice for patients with Dow Corning implants, not *against* plaintiffs' attorneys. As McKennon had initially admonished when he joined Dow Corning, the constructive actions aligned the company with its obligation to breast implant patients. While research completed to date had not supported a connection between breast implants and auto-immune disease, questions had been raised for which answers were needed.

Like John Rowe, Keith McKennon also engaged with stakeholders in developing his platform of constructive actions. Despite the extensive, volatile ongoing litigation, McKennon and CCO Barie Carmichael met with high-profile breast-implant plaintiffs to discuss the concept of a breast implant removal program, with plaintiffs' input directly shaping the program's underlying policies. The meeting was held with the commitment that Dow Corning would seek no external visibility for the meeting. The objective was to ensure the program's policies worked from the perspective of those who would use it. In addition, Dow Corning provided financial support to breast cancer support groups whose telephone hotlines had been flooded with questions about breast implants, not breast cancer. This funding offset the additional telecommunications costs and resources these groups were absorbing, which were diverting them from their core mission of providing support to women with breast cancer.

ASKING UNASKED QUESTIONS

Additionally, McKennon brought his empathetic outside-in perspective when engaging with another group of key stakeholders: employees who were concerned not only about the company but also the implications of a new CEO imported from one of the parent companies, Dow Chemical. Just days after his arrival, McKennon led his first employee forum, a no-questions-barred employee meeting with phone links to locations around the world. Just as he had modeled with the new breast-implant management team, McKennon led by example, publicly asking himself the question that was on everyone's minds but which no one would ask. "If I were you," McKennon said in his down-home, Garrison Keillor–like style, "I'd want to know if this new guy from Dow Chemical was going to transform this company to mirror Dow," surprising, disarming, and then amusing employees with his candor. He told employees that although he was a proud Dow Chemical retiree, he was now an employee and CEO of another great company, Dow Corning, with a unique heritage he would preserve and also with a promising future. He asked his employees to keep serving customers and let the implant team deal with the crisis.

The seeds of change planted from the constructive actions taken in 1992 moved the science on breast implants forward, away from the circus environment of mass tort litigation. Having articulated the constructive next steps toward a solution, the media frenzy stopped nearly immediately. By 1994, a Mayo Clinic study was published showing no risk for connective tissue disease in women with breast implants. By December 1995, more than twenty studies not funded by Dow Corning had been published globally from a variety of institutions, all declaring the same result. By 1996, courts began appointing expert panels to review the science, exercising their judicial gatekeeper responsibility to determine what was admissible, reliable scientific evidence to present to a jury. Plaintiffs' experts who had previously made a lucrative career testifying in breast implant trials were no longer meeting the judicial criteria for qualified experts. Finally, in 1999, at the request of Congress, the prestigious Institute of Medicine (now the National Academy of Medicine) reviewed the science on breast implants and declared that toxicology studies on silicones did not provide a basis for breast implant health concerns, nor did the evidence from epidemiological studies.

The turnaround in the crisis resulted directly from the Dow Corning crisis management team's decisions made and actions taken in 1992. Subsequent Dow Corning CEOs who succeeded Keith McKennon—Richard Hazleton, Gary Anderson, and Stephanie Burns—stayed the course, including through nine years of operating under the protection of a chapter 11 bankruptcy reorganization, which Dow Corning filed to consolidate implant claims under a court-managed resolution process. Customer and supplier support remained solid with no reported business erosion owing to the issue, and key communities where Dow Corning had a large presence stayed supportive. Most significantly, employee survey results showed a bedrock trust in the company, with an average of more than 80 percent saying they were proud to work for Dow Corning in surveys conducted from 1992 until the company's emergence from chapter 11 in 2004. As a testimony to that employee support, over two thousand employees surprised management by raising money to purchase and personally sign a six-page advertisement in a local newspaper following the filing of chapter 11 with the headline, "To Dow Corning Executive Management, Your Employees Are Behind You 100 Percent!"

APPLYING LESSONS LEARNED

Aetna's and Dow Corning's lessons learned in restoring their reputations have important similarities directly applicable in the new social landscape: a multifunctional executive management team with the authority to strategize and implement a platform of constructive solutions leading to a common ground with critics and stakeholders; a strategic pivot from a defensive posture with critics to a position of advocating what the company is for, not what it is against; and a leader and leadership team able to understand the stakeholder perspective, offering a new lens through which the crisis could be understood, managed, and communicated.

A crisis marks an identifiable breach of trust with stakeholders, the breaking of an organization's contract with those who trust it—witness Lance Armstrong's Living Strong with assistance—thus eroding the ability to advance corporate strategy and the company's license to operate. Writing to his son in a famous set of tenth-century letters, Lord Chesterfield advised that "the possession of all the moral virtues . . . is not sufficient . . . you must have the reputation of them also."

Recovering a crisis-damaged reputation requires a long-term perspective that can repair trust, proven through constructive action aligned with stakeholder expectations. Particularly in this new landscape, it requires building relationships forged through stakeholder interactions throughout all levels of the company, going back to basics on the elements of building a Champion Brand: alignment, authenticity, attachment, and advocacy. The process required to restore trust is not all that different from the process required to establish and maintain it. No one should be shocked that the process for restoring trust takes longer and is more challenging.

Given that social media, particularly in the current hyper-polarized environment, elevates the risk of getting unwanted notoriety in a fast-moving crisis, it is even more incumbent upon a corporation to use the transparency afforded in this new landscape to its advantage by creating a web-based track record of its actions to mitigate inherent negatives and advocate solutions benefitting both business and society:

articulating actions that demonstrate shared advocacy; monitoring social media for emerging issues; building relationships with stakeholders and stakebrokers before an issue crests; and engaging in third-party verification of the metrics measuring the company's progress.

The Internet and social media give companies an unprecedented opportunity to articulate, continually update, and engage others. Effective communication can blunt a growing crisis, like blocking a spike in volleyball. Corporations waiting to create a web-based track record until after the "spike" has been hit invite an unforced error with potentially substantial, costly, and time-consuming consequences.

PERIPHERAL VISION

That said, in the supersonic speed of today's social landscape, how a company addresses a trending social issue requires peripheral vision cultivated by a culture and management team with sufficiently diverse perspectives to anticipate stakeholder reactions outside the corporate bubble, comparable to the fresh perspectives Rowe and McKennon brought to their companies. While that may sound obvious, getting perspectives outside of the corporate bubble requires active intervention to overcome the insulating power of corporate group think which too often produces unintentional corporate blind spots. Even companies widely recognized for their actions to address societal needs can have missteps that become instantly viral.

Witness Pepsi's controversial advertisement posted to YouTube featuring Kendall Jenner offering a Pepsi to a police officer during a protest. The advertisement's intended message—unity, peace, and understanding—was in stark contrast to the message received by many vocal critics who saw it as trivializing the real-world experiences of those involved in the serious business of protests against social injustice. In particular, critics saw the advertisement as the antithesis to being "woke" to the societal impediments that confront marginalized people, as captured in the television documentary, *Stay Woke: The Black Lives Matter Movement*.[11]

Since no company is immune to mistakes, the quality of a company's immediate response is key to recovering reputation. "Clearly, we missed the mark, and we apologize," Pepsi said in its statement, clearly acknowledging its mistake and announcing its quick action to remove the YouTube ad and halt any further rollout. Pepsi's fast apology and immediate corrective actions quickly stemmed the social media storm.[12]

While speed is a key factor in this new environment, no reputation was ever advanced by quickly articulating the wrong message. The urgency to quickly issue a tweet, without pausing to consider the context, to assess the issue's relationship or relevance to a business's strategy, priorities, and stakeholders or the business's authenticity as the messenger, can quickly backfire. The need for speed does not trump the requirement for a thoughtful process to assess the appropriate response, if any at all, to the issue.

UNDERSTANDING THE SOCIAL CONTEXT

Informal networks quickly formed on social media spread news that can turn a company like Uber, for example, from an enterprise with the business model of the day into a company with problems. On Saturday, January 28, 2017, at 4:55 PM, a New York City taxi union tweeted that it would stage an impromptu strike for taxi service at John F. Kennedy International Airport (JFK) between 6:00 PM and 7:00 PM in protest of President Trump's executive order temporarily restricting some people from entering the United States. The strike demonstrated solidarity with Muslims, who comprise a substantial segment of taxi and ridesharing drivers. At 7:36 PM, shortly after the taxi strike was to have expired, Uber tweeted that it had temporarily canceled surge pricing for rides to JFK, alerting customers that they may experience longer wait times. "Please be patient," Uber's tweet requested.[13]

The juxtaposition of the two tweets less than three hours apart led many to infer that Uber drivers were acting as scabs in the New York taxi driver strike by undercutting fares, at a time when yellow cab drivers were returning to work at the end of their impromptu strike. Uber's initial tweet, combined with what many saw as Uber CEO Travis Kalanick's mild criticism of President Trump's executive order, led to the hashtag #DeleteUber, which went viral with users and celebrities deleting their Uber apps. Given the well-known conflicts between taxi drivers and ridesharing companies like Uber, particularly in New York City, an outside-in stakeholder perspective should have anticipated this reaction.

In the new social landscape with its instant reactions, tone deafness to the broader social context is dangerous and likely to trigger immediate reactions, as Pepsi discovered and quickly remedied.

Uber's attempt to recover from the growing negative reaction included a series of new constructive actions and commitments: compensating any drivers unable to return to the United States during the travel ban to ensure their families would not be left without income; establishing a $3 million legal defense fund to help its drivers with immigration and translation services; replying to customers who had deleted the Uber app asking them to reconsider and mentioning some of the constructive actions taken to support drivers affected by the ban; and posting Kalanick's letter to Uber staff on Facebook, in which he committed to addressing the issue at President Trump's first business advisory group meeting. Kalanick's message, however, neither referenced the #DeleteUber movement nor acknowledged the company's missteps that led to the movement, as Pepsi had done in acknowledging its mistake to stem the reaction to its YouTube advertisement. Uber's actions and statements did not quiet the outrage; Uber's website continued to be flooded with complaints. Hours after its initial tweet regarding the waiving of surge pricing, Uber apologized "for any confusion about our earlier tweet—it was not meant to break up any strike."[14]

Demonstrating in real time the primacy of actions over statements in the new social landscape, Uber drivers operating to and from JFK without surge pricing during the controversy trumped the effectiveness of the company's mitigating statements. For many critics, Uber's actions in the taxi strike were consistent with previous corporate actions that critics felt exploited a situation for profit, like charging surge pricing during Hurricane Sandy. Uber's business model of dynamic supply-versus-demand rideshare pricing had run into the inherent negatives embedded in that model when operating in a unique social context. During a disaster, as in the case of Hurricane Sandy, applying surge pricing could be seen as price gouging. During a strike to protest a perceived bias against Muslims, as in the case of the impromptu New York City taxi strike, lifting the price surge could be seen as trying to undercut competing taxi drivers. In both cases, Uber's pricing policies were seen as exploiting unique circumstances for profit. In today's dramatically changed relationship between business and society, policies and actions must be assessed through the outside-in lens of societal and stakeholder impact. A decade later, the lessons learned from Aetna's and Dow Corning's strategies to regain their reputations are immediately applicable but are being played out in the new landscape's unprecedented volume and velocity.

Uber's response to the New York taxi strike provided a market lift for one of its competitors, Lyft, which continued to serve JFK but did not turn off its surge pricing following the taxi strike. Instead, Lyft waited to react until the following morning, when cofounder and CEO Logan Green issued tweets strongly critical of the president's executive order, calling it "antithetical to both Lyft's and our nation's core values."[15] The company also committed to donating $1 million over the next four years to the American Civil Liberties Union to defend the Constitution. Some have questioned the real impact Lyft's donation would have, but Green's more strongly worded statement on President Trump's executive order, as compared to Uber's initial responses, made headlines. The following day, for the first time, user downloads of the Lyft app surpassed those for Uber.[16]

The taxi strike controversy was far from being a bet-the-company-crisis. Uber will likely recover from its actions following Trump's travel ban, given the attachment it has built to its brand, unless the root cause for the missteps involves a more chronic problem with its business management. But the incident and the contrast in response between Uber and Lyft combine to provide a teachable moment for doing business in this era. The new landscape has exponentially compressed the time for an issue to gain a critical mass of visibility and has also given companies tools to quickly address the situation. But the dynamics of high-volume visibility and unprecedented velocity do not overtake the need to understand the real or perceived social impact of considered policies and actions. Taking a pause, even in this new environment, to assess actions relative to the business' vision, values, and strategies is time well spent. Critical to Aetna's and Dow Corning's reputation recovery, the insight gained from considering policies and actions using peripheral vision through a stakeholder lens is even more important today, as the urge to respond quickly can overtake the need to respond appropriately.

7

RESETTING THE SWEET SPOT

This book began with the premise that a new landscape has fundamentally reset the relationship between business and society requiring strategic C-suite-level management solutions anchored in an outside-in understanding of the stakeholder footprint of the business model itself. Fundamental to this reset is the widening gap between the public's long-eroding trust in business and their growing expectations for businesses to make positive contributions to society.

Just as important has been the collapse of barriers for the public's voice to be heard. Quickly forming and morphing communities of thought, armed with mobile devices and social media platforms, are exercising unprecedented global scrutiny of the corporation itself, not just its products. Stakebrokers are the new loci of power and influence, ranging from impassioned, engaged, web-savvy citizens to well-known but equally web-savvy public figures. They can marshal legions of followers and generate multiplier-effect "shares" to move an issue from a standing start to a global movement, disrupting business strategies.

People are watching. Everything.

THE RISK OF COMPLACENCY

Eroding trust has not been limited to business. Declining trust in institutions, once taken for granted, has created a new normal of unpredictability. Mainstream news media, subject to changes in communication technology, have seen their business model transformed. For many, mainstream media no longer represent a platform to enable consensus or even a range of trusted opinion or reliable fact. In fact, the very definition of what *is* a fact is amazingly a matter of debate.

In the fragmented world of social media, a consensus source of reliable information has evaporated, accelerating both polarization and volatility. Real-time swings in what is urgent and "trending" are the norm. Trust in government has plummeted, though not having far to fall, as a democratic system of checks and balances is no longer the means through which once mundane functions of government are fulfilled. The collective loss of trust in large institutions adds to the already formidable task faced by individual corporations of regaining enough trust to continue to operate, to implement strategy.

Early in this book, we pointed out that modern business was made possible by the work of Enlightenment mathematicians on probability. Still, John Maynard Keynes's skepticism about predicting the future with certainty and Nassim

Nicholas Taleb's black swan theory are healthy correctives to our over-reliance on predictive models. Only after the fact do we confer genius on those who could see the obvious when all about them could not. Where the record companies saw a threat to their business in Napster, Steve Jobs saw the opportunity of iTunes and the iPod. He also saw the far larger sales potential of cellphones compared to personal computers, and so the iPhone was born.

For a decade, Winston Churchill warned against German rearmament. Again, in retrospect, the facts and consequences of not predicting this painfully find the appeasers who opposed him at best lacking in moral fiber. In a less cataclysmic example, Billy Beane took advantage of insights from Sabermetrics to predict that a walk is as good as a base hit. If genius is an unrealistic goal for day-to-day management, finding ways to see predictive trends is perhaps more attainable if the increased volume of accessible information can provide texture and propel the older notion of environmental scanning toward finer-grained insights.

However, even with the new ability to scan the interconnected geopolitical world that business now navigates, access to more information does not ensure C-suite management will have a clearer view to anticipate disruptions to their business. An outside-in perspective does not come naturally to business cultures that are susceptible to groupthink. The biggest risk is complacency. A company can too easily assume it has already identified all of its inherent negatives, even though data clearly show that most corporate crises come from smoldering issues derived from a firm's leadership or management decisions rather than due to a sudden crisis in which the firm has virtually no control or limited responsibility. As a result, even organizations that have mitigated the negative stakeholder impact from some of their operations can still have smoldering inherent negatives that go unnoticed until an event or, at the extreme, a debilitating crisis creates a corporate whack on the side of the head. Suddenly, the strategic surprise becomes a blinding glimpse of the obvious.

Google may promise "Don't be evil," but the strategic surprise of fake news exposed an inherent negative in its business model that incentivized the proliferation of fake news. The fast-casual dining chain Chipotle promised "food with integrity," but had multiple outbreaks of *E. coli* that spread across its stores nationwide. They relied on reasserting their commitment to fresh ingredients rather than persuading customers that they had found the remedy for the breakdown of their supply chain. As in the earlier Odwalla crisis, where tainted apple juice led to fatalities, the company felt armored by the noble intent of using organic ingredients. Odwalla finally instituted a remedy, "flash pasteurization," in 1996 and is now one of Coca-Cola's brands. Selling organic fresh food in an expanding supply chain or expanding a brand selling organic juice should have exposed a potential inherent negative in the business model that comes with the possibility of less certainty about food safety. This could and should have been anticipated, with solutions enacted.

The need for a forward-leaning corporate culture that anticipates stakeholder impact has never been more urgent. Today the ramp time for smoldering stakeholder issues to morph into a movement is short, if not instant. We live at a moment when public opinion on key issues has flipped to top of mind after years of latent concern, when issues directly and often immediately impact sales and profit, as well as the relevance and viability of iconic brands. Natural foods have been around for a while—as has the paleo diet—and a penchant for artisanal goat cheese melted on organic sourdough has no doubt been attainable in Sonoma and lower Manhattan for a good while. But it would have been hard to predict just when a grilled cheese on white bread became hazardous to one's health. However, it was not in time to prevent the merger of Heinz and Kraft. Just a few years ago, it would have been hard to anticipate that the Internet of things integrating Wi-Fi into everyday devices and appliances like televisions, refrigerators, and home security systems could become instruments for the invasion of consumer privacy when highjacked by cyber monitoring.

A NEW EXECUTIVE LEADERSHIP MINDSET

Anticipating stakeholder impact in this new era requires ongoing vigilance as a way of doing business, but understanding that impact can be illusive. In their thought-provoking report, *Thinking the Unthinkable*, authors Nik Gowing and Chris Langdon interviewed 60 prominent corporate, public service, and political leaders regarding new vulnerabilities they are facing. The majority of those interviewed argued that today's speed of change requires new executive leadership skills to anticipate strategic surprises. In particular, the executives interviewed warned of a leadership aversion to address "unpalatable" risks to their business, creating a "willful blindness" to disruptive trends obvious to some, particularly millennials. Leaders "are not recruiting enough people with a different vision who are out of the box," summed up one chief executive.[1] Anticipating disruptions in this new social landscape requires C-suite leaders with the skills to ask the right questions and frame the key problems while also recruiting and rewarding responsible skeptics in their organizations to do the same. Corporate leaders can make it politically safe to ask uncomfortable questions and raise troublesome concerns. Creating that culture starts at the top.

Equally important is seeding a C-suite management team with individuals who bring diverse perspectives, both by their personal disposition and their management responsibilities. Executive leaders whose business responsibilities inherently require a stakeholder line of sight, particularly the chief executives leading corporate affairs, communications, and talent management, must sit with key operational leaders at the executive management table. In this new era, power has shifted to web-enabled internal and external stakeholders, usurping management's full control of their messaging, corporate narratives, and brand. With engaged stakeholders forming alliances and acting at the speed of thought both externally and internally, the insights of executives leading corporate affairs, communications, and talent management—whose positions are centered on understanding internal and external stakeholders—are fundamental to the diverse perspectives required for businesses to success-fully navigate this new landscape.

Millennials, who are becoming the majority in a com-pany's workforce as baby boomers retire, are vigilant inter-nal watchdogs of consistency, quick to flag when corporate actions disconnect from a company's publicly stated values. If companies are lucky, employees will address the discon-nect internally and drive constructive changes in policy and actions, as was the case with fake news at Facebook. But as IBM and Oracle discovered, those employees can also resign, publicly, in protest with those actions becoming trending news. In this new landscape, authenticity is not only criti-cal to public and customer perceptions of product or service brands, but also to corporate brands and a corporation's abil-ity to remain competitive by attracting and retaining its next generation of leaders.

THINKING OUTSIDE OF THE FOUR WALLS

Companies who are adapting to the reset in the relationship between business and society cultivate an outside-in cul-ture that proactively seeks to understand and anticipate the stakeholder impact of their business models. Here we mean a kind of literacy or fluency in the broader implications of the business model. It requires an ability to think outside of what is often called the "four walls" of the company to anticipate the stakeholder impact of corporate strategies, governance, and policies with the result being corporate actions taken and decisions made.

Blue Cross and Blue Shield (BCBS), for example, has partnered with ridesharing company Lyft to increase health care access for its members in communities with "transportation deserts." By thinking outside of the "four walls" of medical claims processing, BCBS can improve the health of its 106 million members by identifying at the zip-code level the community factors that have the most dramatic impact on individual health, clearly a win–win for both BCBS and its members. "Many Americans live in areas where medical care is beyond the reach of walking, biking, or public transportation. As a result, they struggle to access critical health care services, even when they have health insurance," explains Dr. Trent Haywood, BCBS America chief medical officer and President of BCBS Institute which addresses the social determinants of health at the community level.[2] The partnership with Lyft initiated in 2017 enables free rides to medical appointments for BCBS plan holders who lack reliable transportation, without requiring a smartphone Lyft app. The rides, a covered benefit, are set up through the doctor's office.[3]

The BCBS example clearly shows the upside value of thinking outside the "four walls" to anticipate how corporate strategies and polices affect stakeholders. Conversely, failure to develop this outside-in perspective can lead to tone deaf policies and actions, no matter how unintentional, instantly displayed on social media. United Airlines' policies regarding "re-accommodating" a passenger bumped from a flight, resulting in a video posted on social media that went viral showing an unwilling paying passenger being dragged off the plane, is a vivid example.[4] Other airlines likely went to school on the implications for their own policies, with United's experience providing the wakeup call. Beyond the customer impact of overbooking policies, the United example raises questions about policies governing the degree of discretion given to gate agents and crew on implementing the policy as well as the policies for repositioning crews who could displace paying customers.

The inability to think outside of the four walls to understand stakeholder impact can also apply to an entire industry, as technology writer Om Malik observed in his *New Yorker* article "Silicon Valley Has an Empathy Vacuum." "It's hard to think about the human consequence of technology as a founder of a startup racing to prove itself or as a chief executive who is worried about the incessant growth that keeps investors happy," he writes. "However, when you are a data-driven oligarchy like Facebook, Google, Amazon or Uber, you can't really wash your hands of the impact of your algorithms and your ability to shape popular sentiment in our society. We are not just talking about the ability to influence voters with fake news. If you are Amazon, you have to acknowledge that you are slowly corroding the retail sector, which employs many people in this country. If you are Airbnb, no matter how well-meaning your focus on delighting travelers, you are also going to affect hotel-industry employment."[5] Malik cautions that unless the tech industry can anticipate its societal impact on those whom it threatens, the tech industry could overtake Wall Street as a lead villain in popular imagination.

"WE" RATHER THAN "I"

Adopting a wider field of vision to think outside of the "four walls" of the company is a shared characteristic of the corporations profiled in chapter 5, "The New Corporate Branding." This has led some business leaders to recognize that their companies cannot by themselves solve the pressing issues impacting both their own businesses and society. As one chief executive interviewed by Nik Gowing and Chris Langdon put it, "We are seeing the rise of the new 'humble CEO,' someone who talks about 'we' rather than 'I.' "[6] The challenges are too large and complex, requiring "we" solutions through businesses, governments, and the public sector working collectively. In *Corporation 2020*, environmental economist Pavan Sukhdev argues a similar point on the need for collective, collaborative solutions that recognize interdependencies and common interests. He advocates for private finance and private companies to drive a green economy, but also feels that government "has an important role to play" through taxation policies and "catalysts." [7]

Similarly, Andy Grove, whose anecdote on the Pentium bug crisis started this book, in 2010 warned Silicon Valley of the future negative consequences of what he saw as the tech industry's widening disconnect with society. In his view, the industry had forfeited its competitive edge by not using its innovations and wealth to foster job growth in the United States and by not investing in the American workforce to nurture the next generation of innovators. He wrote that government should set priorities for job creation and business should operate not only with immediate profit in mind but also in the "interests of employees, and employees yet to be hired."[8] With a similar perspective, Muhtar Kent, CEO of Coca-Cola, speaks of a golden triangle made up of the public, private enterprise, and government.[9]

In the now permanently interconnected world, the public, private enterprises, and governments collectively face complex challenges. As a result, the more than thirty-year cycle of placing government in opposition to the private sector is long past its sell-by date. If the rationale is that, excepting the armed forces, the government cannot do anything, why do UPS and FedEx sometimes use the United States Postal Service as a carrier?

At the other extreme, political candidates of both major parties, with varying degrees of credibility and sincerity, bash "big corporations" and "Wall Street" to elicit reliable applause. However, a good many corporations have in place, or are trending toward, positions on social issues and employees that are well ahead of political debate or policy goals. In advance of the 2017 G7 Summit in Italy, chief executives of leading U.S. companies collectively signed letters and purchased full-page newspaper advertisements urging President Trump to support America's continued involvement in the Paris Climate Agreement, saying the agreement benefits American companies, suppliers, customers, and communities.[10] Concerns regarding immigration and national security were factors in electing Donald Trump president of the United States. Yet business leaders have taken a visible lead in articulating the critical role immigrants play in advancing American prosperity and innovation. Tesla CEO Elon Musk, for example, has articulated the tech industry's need for specialized talent; the CEO of Cargill, David MacLennan, testified in Congress on the essential labor pool refugees and immigrants provide to business operations in the United States. According to the United States Census Bureau, immigrants hold 35 percent of the country's 441,000 meat-processing jobs, including refugees from East Africa.[11] At a grassroots level, February 15 has become the "Day Without Immigrants," when many immigrants in major cities stay home from work or school to tangibly demonstrate their critical role in the nation's economy and social structure. Many shops and restaurants close in solidarity while others prepare for operational shutdowns owing to insufficient staff.

Similarly, food and beverage companies like Mars, Nestlé, and PepsiCo have engaged in initiatives with the nonprofit Partnership for a Healthier America (PHA) to address growing social concerns with issues like obesity and diabetes to improve the nutritional content of their foods. Many of the PHA partnerships are binding legal contracts with independent third parties monitoring compliance. Ironically, this progress continues as the federal government rolls back previously enacted nutritional rules and regulations. "Washington is Washington, but progress will continue," commented PHA CEO Larry Solar to the *Washington Post*. "We're proving the private sector can play as big a role as policy change."[12]

PRESERVING LATENT GOODWILL

Despite the disruptive challenges posed by a web-enabled public, people who grew up with iconic product brands do not want them to go away. If that sounds dissonant at a time when corporations in the aggregate have engendered so much mistrust, the attachment to iconic product brands may provide a reservoir of goodwill, or latent goodwill, for the corporate brand in this era of increasing corporate scrutiny. Iconic brands are a part of our culture, and many have been around for more than or close to a century. It seems reasonable to argue that beyond the benefit of the doubt, many consumers do not want to see iconic brands vanish if the companies do what they can to address their corporate brand concerns. People want to have a Coke or Pepsi with a hamburger or slice of pizza occasionally. Even many green tea–drinkers most likely want the option to buy, for example, a pair of Levi's made by a company once derided for not moving production offshore soon enough. Now, for $128, you can buy a pair of Levi's made in America to join a closet full of once-everyday brands now priced as luxury goods if they are made in America.

Consumer-facing companies have not taken the goodwill reservoir for their product or service brands for granted. As many of the examples cited in this book demonstrate, they are actively addressing the alignment and authenticity elements of their corporate brands and building attachment by addressing inherent negatives in their business models, whether owing to the stakeholder impact of their supply chains or in matters of corporate policies or governance. They are building attachment through business strategies that integrate profit with a corporate purpose, engaging with society in shared advocacy to solve problems common to their business and society.

To illustrate how quickly this has changed, in 2011 Steve Jobs exemplified Andy Grove's criticism of Silicon Valley's disconnect with society when he bluntly told then-President Obama that Apple's manufacturing jobs "aren't coming back" to the United States. At the time, Tim Cook, then Apple's operations expert, led the preference for manufacturing Apple devices in Asia. The issue was less a matter of low-cost manufacturing labor than about the speed and flexibility of Asia's supply chains. The United States, Cook declared in 2012 as Apple's new CEO, "can't compete at this point."[13]

In 2017, just five years later, Asia's manufacturing supply chain likely still held its speed and flexibility advantage over the United States, yet Cook announced Apple's new $1 billion fund to promote advanced manufacturing jobs in the United States. Likely the social unrest among U.S. middle-class manufacturing workers that helped catalyze the election of Donald Trump at least partially prompted this new initiative. Whatever the myriad of causes, Cook's 2017 comments on Apple's role in creating jobs contrast substantially with his remarks made in 2012: "A lot of people ask me, 'Do you think it's a company's job to create jobs?' and my response is [that] a company should have values because a company is a collection of people. And people should have values, so by extension a company should. And one of the things you do is give back," Cook explained in 2017. "So how do you give back? We give back through our work in the environment, in running the company on renewable energy. We give back in job creation."[14]

"AN ECONOMIC ECOSYSTEM"

Beyond consumer-product companies, corporations like GE and IBM have adopted new corporate-brand taglines that serve as kernels for new corporate narratives, building an attachment to a corporate brand earned through strategic decisions and actions that benefit both their businesses and society. As centenarian-plus companies, both GE (founded in 1892) and IBM (founded in 1911) have had to reinvent themselves over their history, as new business models or technologies have disrupted their legacy high-margin businesses. While new enterprises can innovate from a clean slate, established enterprises like GE and IBM must find new sources of revenue while legacy business pays the light bill. This has always been a classic balancing act in business, sometimes engendering restless investors anxious for faster growth. Both companies have experienced some degree of investor unrest, but both have stayed the course with long-term financial growth strategies, Smarter Planet (IBM) and Ecomagination (GE), that also benefit society. At its ten-year anniversary, Ecomagination had generated more than $200 billion in revenues.[15] In her 2016 annual report letter to investors, Ginni Rometty, IBM's CEO, announced that IBM's strategic imperatives had reached critical mass, generating 41 percent of its overall revenues in 2016 at $33 billion.

In Jeff Immelt's 2016 remarks to graduates of New York University's Stern School of Business, he observed the dramatically changed environment driving fundamental changes in how successful businesses must now operate. In the current volatile global economy with its increasing rejection of globalization in favor of protectionist policies, "Companies must navigate the world on their own," Immelt declared. "We must level the playing field without government engagement. This requires dramatic transformation." In fact, business is sometimes better positioned to affect the changes needed, both for its own success and society's. "Sometimes business can drive change faster than government," he remarked. "It is tough to hate a company that is reducing climate change and creating jobs."[16]

The solution, said Immelt, requires a long-term view to see the win–win opportunities. "Our goal is to build an economic ecosystem that is the most competitive in the world. To create great jobs through private enterprise and ingenuity. To give back competency and innovation directed at solving the world's toughest problems."[17]

RESETTING THE SWEET SPOT

In a previous era, navigating a successful business meant finding the sweet spot where a customer's unmet need and a product or service intersected. Today, that intersection is more complex but still navigable. It means adding a third circle to the previous two-circle Venn diagram. In the new social landscape, a corporate product or service must still intersect with a customer's unmet need. But the distinguishing sweet spot adds meeting a societal need, creating a three-way intersection: Delivering a product or service that meets a customer's needs through profitable business strategies that also benefit society.

In this three-way intersection, a business must still be profitable. Even in business ethics, a business case must be made: costs saved from avoiding scandals rooted in unethical cultures; supply chain improvements that both reduce cost and mitigate negative stakeholder impact; value and business growth created through the win–win solutions. In the three-way intersection of customer need, business capability, and societal need, business must have a clear stake in the social needs it addresses. What has not changed in this new landscape is the need to be profitable. What has changed is web-enabled stakeholder vigilance for how that profit is made.

For B corporations, the sweet spot of a profitable product or service meeting a customer need in a way that also benefits society is fundamental to its entire business. In Warby Parker's "buy one, give one" business model, for example, each pair of eyeglasses purchased means another pair given to the nonprofit VisionSpring, which then sells the glasses in developing countries to build entrepreneurship. Warby Parker also donates glasses to people in need.

Beyond that unique category of business, corporations are increasingly adopting business strategies that create this three-way sweet spot where business, customer needs, and societal needs intersect. The breadth of that sweet spot varies. At one end of the spectrum, companies are actively addressing societal needs through proactively mitigating the stakeholder impact of their business model's inherent negatives. In this new era, mitigating negative stakeholder impact is a threshold requirement. It is a predicate to building a sustainable corporate reputation and brand.

Some corporations have broadened the three-way intersection by going beyond mitigating just their specific business's negative stakeholder impact. They are also convening a diverse community of stakeholders and other businesses to jointly discover new platforms of shared advocacy. They are mitigating the negative stakeholder impacts of multiple businesses, for example sharing supply chain operational solutions across their industry to stem the depletion of dwindling, vital natural resources. Their objective is to leverage their collective scale to magnify their joint impact in addressing a broad societal challenge in which their businesses and society have a shared, direct stake. In the process, businesses and stakeholders, including nongovernmental organizations, are learning from each other, replacing perhaps formerly held stereotypes with substantive, mutually beneficial relationships in a shared advocacy, as the examples of Patagonia, Unilever, and Waste Management illustrate.

Others have built an even wider three-way intersection through a platform of shared advocacy to unlock the long-term business growth opportunities inherent to directing their competencies and innovation at solving some of the world's toughest problems, as GE's Jeff Immelt described in his Stern School of Business address.

Regardless of where a business is positioned in this new spectrum, the era of the "either–or" business paradigm—a core mission of financial returns to investors as the exclusive business mandate—is being replaced by "both–and"—with companies proactively seeking business strategies that address the unmet needs of their customers as well as the enlightened self-interests of *both* business *and* society.

This new era's "sweet spot" is where the needs of the customer, business, and society intersect. Businesses finding that sweet spot are building trust and meeting the rising expectations for business in the new social landscape.

NOTES

FOREWORD

1. "Industrial Statesmanship," October 27, 1939, http://bellisario .psu.edu/page-assets/assets/pdf/page_speech_archive.pdf.
2. *The Dynamics of Public Trust in Business*, Arthur W. Page Society and Business Roundtable Institute for Corporate Ethics, https://docs.google.com/gview?url=https://awpagesociety .com/attachments/26223e991691cb3ae9ac764d6859fc1c148d 423f/store/8099fa44e4401bda4afec29a36050afb3fddaf2e2faa c3944bf5771182ea/Full_Report.pdf.
3. Popularized by John Mackey, Whole Foods cofounder and co-CEO; and Raj Sisodia, professor of marketing at Bentley University, through their book, *Conscious Capitalism: Liberating the Heroic Spirit of Business* (Boston, MA: Harvard Business School, 2012), http://www.investopedia.com/terms/c /conscious-capitalism.asp.
4. "Shared value is not social responsibility, philanthropy, or sustainability, but a new way for companies to achieve economic success." Michael E. Porter and Mark Kramer, "Creating Shared Value," *Harvard Business Review*. http://sharedvalue.org/about -shared-value.

INTRODUCTION

1. Andrew S. Grove, *Only the Paranoid Survive: How to Exploit the Crisis Points that Challenge Every Company* (New York: Random House, 1999).
2. "Reaching 50 Million Users," *Visually*, May 1, 2012, http://visual.ly/reaching-50-million-users.
3. Christopher Grant, "Pokémon Go Has Been Downloaded 50 Million Times," *Polygon*, September 7, 2016, http://www.polygon.com/pokemon-go/2016/9/7/12836898/pokemon-go-downloads-500-million.
4. Patricia E. Dowden and Philip M. Nichols, "Stakeholder Trust: A Business Case," *The Compliance and Ethics Blog*, August 11, 2015, http://complianceandethics.org/stakeholder-trust-a-business-case/.
5. Bidhan L. Parmar and Laura Hennessey Martens, "What Makes a Champion Brand? Ten Champion Brand Survey Insights Every Business Leader Needs to Know," *Darden Ideas to Action*, March 16, 2015, https://ideas.darden.virginia.edu/2015/03/what-makes-a-champion-brand-ten-champion-brand-survey-insights-every-business-leader-needs-to-know/.
6. "An Interview with BP's Head of Crisis Communications," *Phoebesreel*, August 31, 2011, https://phoebesreel.wordpress.com/2011/08/31/an-interview-with-bps-head-of-crisis-communications/.
7. Alan Mascarenhas, "BP's Global PR vs. BPGlobalPR," *Newsweek*, June 3, 2010, http://www.newsweek.com/bps-global-pr-vs-bpglobalpr-73125.
8. "BP Spills Coffee (Sketch Comedy Parody by UCB)," YouTube video, 2:48, posted by Mike Gillett Comedy, posted November 9, 2014, https://www.youtube.com/watch?v=ojw_oq87iGs.

1. THE BUSINESS TRUST–EXPECTATIONS GAP

1. "Confidence in Institutions," Gallup, Inc., June 2016, www.gallup.com/poll/1597/confidence-institutions.aspx.

2. Ibid.

3. Kent Hoover, "Public Opinion of Big Business Improves, But Small Business Still Rules," *The Business Journals*, August 5, 2014, www.bizjournals.com/bizjournals/washingtonbureau/2014/08/public-opinion-of-big-business-improves-but-small.html.

4. "2015 Public Affairs Pulse Survey: Most Americans Say It's Smart for Big Companies to Get Political," Public Affairs Council, September 10, 2015, http://pac.org/news/general/most-americans-say-its-smart-for-big-companies-to-get-political.

5. Bidhan L. Parmar and Laura Hennessey Martens, "What Makes a Champion Brand? Ten Champion Brand Survey Insights Every Business Leader Needs to Know," *Darden Ideas to Action*, March 16, 2015, https://ideas.darden.virginia.edu/2015/03/what-makes-a-champion-brand-ten-champion-brand-survey-insights-every-business-leader-needs-to-know/. "What Makes a Champion Brand?"

   Champion Brand was a survey of the general public in Brazil, Canada, China, France, Germany, Hong Kong, India, Italy, Japan, Mexico, Russia, Spain, the United Kingdom, and the United States. The survey was conducted via an online panel, and thus its respondents should be considered to make up unbiased samples in developing and developed countries.

6. Parmar and Martens, "What Makes a Champion Brand?"

7. "Ecomagination," General Electric, accessed July 15, 2017, www.ge.com/about-us/ecomagination.

8. Campbell Robertson and John Schwartz, "How a Gulf Settlement that BP Once Hailed Became Its Target," *New York Times*, April 26, 2014, www.nytimes.com/2014/04/27/us/how-a-gulf-settlement-that-bp-once-hailed-became-its-target.html?_r=0.

9. Jeffrey Gottfried and Elisa Shearer, "News Use Across Social Media Platforms 2016," Pew Research Center, May 26, 2016, www.journalism.org/2016/05/26/news-use-across-social-media-platforms-2016/?utm_content=bufferae870&utm

_medium=social&utm_source=twitter.com&utm_campaign
=buffer.

10. Jason Abbruzzese, "Donald Trump provides much-needed spark for investigative journalism," Mashable, January 24, 2017, http://mashable.com/2017/01/24/trump-investigative-journalism/#Au540q7SOaq4/.

2. CLOSING THE GAP IN THE NEW SOCIAL LANDSCAPE

1. Mark Fainaru-Wada and Steve Fainaru, *League of Denial*, (New York: Crown, 2013); PBS Frontline investigative film October 8, 2013; http://www.pbs.org/wgbh/frontline/film/league-of-denial/, accessed July 8, 2017; *NPR Morning Edition*, "When It Comes to Brain Injury, Authors Say NFL is in a 'League of Denial,'" October 7, 2013, http://www.npr.org/2013/10/07/229181970/when-it-comes-to-brain-injury-authors-say-nfl-is-in-a-league-of-denial.

2. Brian Stelter, "The secrets of David Fahrenthold's reporting on the Trump Foundation," CNN, September 14, 2016.

3. Edward Broughton, "The Bhopal Disaster and Its Aftermath: A Review," *Environmental Health* 4, no. 6, May 10, 2005, http://ehjournal.biomedcentral.com/articles/10.1186/1476-069X-4-6.

4. Daniel Gilbert and Justin Schleck, "BP Is Found Grossly Negligent in Deepwater Horizon Disaster," *Wall Street Journal*, September 4, 2014, https://www.wsj.com/articles/u-s-judge-finds-bp-grossly-negligent-in-2010-deepwater-horizon-disaster-1409842182?mg=prod/accounts-wsj.

5. Tara Parker-Pope, "How Parents Harnessed the Power of Social Media to Challenge EpiPen Prices," *New York Times*, August 25, 2016, https://well.blogs.nytimes.com/2016/08/25/how-parents-harnessed-the-power-of-social-media-to-challenge-epipen-prices/.

6. Ibid.

7. Katie Thomas, "Mylan to Settle EpiPen Overpricing Case for $465 Million," *New York Times*, October 7, 2016, https://www.nytimes.com/2016/10/08/business/epipen-mylan-justice-department-settlement.html.

8. Katie Thomas, "Painted as EpiPen Villain, Mylan's Chief Says She Is No Such Thing," *New York Times*, August 26, 2016, https://www.nytimes.com/2016/08/27/business/painted-as-a-villain-mylans-chief-says-shes-no-such-thing.html.

9. Heather Long, "Here's What Happened to AIDS Drug that Spiked 5,000 Percent," *CNN Money*, August 25, 2016, http://money.cnn.com/2016/08/25/news/economy/daraprim-aids-drug-high-price/.

10. Parker-Pope, "How Parents Harnessed the Power of Social Media."

11. Barbara Brooks Kimmel, "Enduring Brands Build Trust Through Actions," LinkedIn, March 14, 2106, https://www.linkedin.com/pulse/enduring-brands-build-trust-through-actions-barbara-brooks-kimmel.

12. Sarab Kochhar, Institute for Public Relations, "Corporate Reputation Takeaways: Results from the 2015 Public Affairs Pulse Survey," September 23, 2015, http://www.instituteforpr.org/corporate-reputation-takeaways-results-from-the-2015-public-affairs-pulse-survey/.

13. Edward D. Hess, *The Road to Organic Growth: How Great Companies Consistently Grow Marketshare from Within* (New York: McGraw-Hill, 2007).

14. Nathan Bomey, "CVS Targets EpiPen with Cheaper, Generic Version," *USA Today*, January 12, 2017, https://www.usatoday.com/story/money/2017/01/12/cvs-health-mylan-epipen-injector-impax-adrenaclick-donald-trump/96479776/.

15. The Authentic Enterprise, http://www.awpagesociety.com/thought-leadership/authentic-enterprise-report; Building Belief, http://www.awpagesociety.com/thought-leadership/building-belief.

16. Margaret Badore, "Starbucks says it now serves '99 percent ethically sourced coffee.' So what does that mean?" Treehugger, April 9, 2015, https://www.treehugger.com/corporate -responsibility/starbucks-says-it-now-serves-99-percent -ethically-sourced-coffee-so-what-does-mean.html.

17. John Elkington, *Cannibals with Forks: The Triple Bottom Line of 21st Century Business* (Stoney Creek, CT: New Society, 1998). Triple-bottom-line reporting suggests that in addition to reporting on profits, companies should report on their impact on people and the planet.

18. Elizabeth Flock, "China Now Has a Fake Ikea Store: When Will We All Stop Copying?" *Washington Post*, August 2, 2011, https:// www.washingtonpost.com/blogs/blogpost/post/china-now -has-fake-ikea-store-when-will-we-all-stop-copying/2011/08/02 /gIQAnVzppI_blog.html?utm_term=.9bb8604497b7.

19. James R. Rubin, Mary Jo Hatch, and Majken Schultz, "Reviewing the Nissan Brand," Case Reference Number UVA-BC-0194 (Charlottesville, VA: Darden Business Publishing, 2006).

20. Linda Du and James McGregor, "The Four Principles of Building Champion Brands: What China Needs to Know to Realize this Goal," *Harvard Business Review China*, September 2013, https://www.scribd.com/document/169231558/The-Four -Principles-of-Building-Champion-Brands-What-China -Needs-to-Know-to-Realize-this-Goal.

21. Bryan Dumont, "Champion Brands Build Greater Shareholder Value," *APCO Forum*, June 5, 2013, http://apcoworldwide .com/blog/detail/apcoforum/2013/06/05/champion-brands -build-greater-shareholder-value.

22. "Patagonia's Mission Statement," Patagonia, http://www .patagonia.com/company-info.html.

23. Council for Textile Recycling, "Wear. Donate. Recycle," WearDonateRecycle.org, http://www.weardonaterecycle.org/.

24. Marc Gunther, "Pressure Mounts to Reform Our Throwaway Culture," *Yale Environment 360*, August 9, 2016, http://e360

.yale.edu/features/pressure_mounts_reform_throw-away
_clothing_culture_hm_recycling.

25. James R. Rubin and Barbara Carmichael, "UPS and Corporate Sustainability: Proactively Managing Risk," Case Reference Number UVA BC-0213 (Charlottesville, VA: Darden Business Publishing, 2007). Unless otherwise stated, all material in this chapter has been sourced from this case study.

3. INHERENT NEGATIVES: MANAGING RISK AND REPUTATION

1. Peter L. Bernstein, *Against the Gods: The Remarkable Story of Risk* (Hoboken, NJ: Wiley, 1998), 2.

2. Ram Charan, *Owning Up: The 14 Questions Every Board Member Needs to Ask*," (San Francisco: Wiley, 2009), 23.

3. "Managing Non-Technical Risk in Exploration and Production (EP) Projects: Opportunity to Leverage the IA Process," IAIA 16 Conference Proceedings, May 11–14, 2016, http://conferences.iaia.org/2016/Final-Papers/Adekoya,%20Adebanji %20-%20Managing%20Non-Technical%20Risk%20in %20E%20and%20P%20Projects.pdf.

4. Institute for Crisis Management, *ICM Annual Crisis Report: News Coverage of Business Crises in 2015*, March 2016, ICM-Annual-Crisis-Report-for-2015.Issued_March22, 2016. http://crisisconsultant.com/wp-content/uploads/2014/11/ICM -Annual-Crisis-Report-for-2015.Issued_March22.2016.pdf.

5. Erika Hayes James and Lynn Perry Wooten, "Crisis Leadership and Why It Matters," *European Financial Review*, December–January 2011.

6. Michael E. Porter and Mark R. Kramer, "The Big Idea: Creating Shared Value," *Harvard Business Review*, January–February 2011.

7. Ibid.

8. Ibid.

9. Andrew Crane and Dirk Matten, "Four Big Problems with 'Creating Shared Value,'" *Crane and Matten Blog* (blog), March 4, 2014, http://craneandmatten.blogspot.ca/2014/03/four-big -problems-with-creating-shared.html.

10. Alexandra Wexler, "Chocolate Makers Fight a Melting Supply of Cocoa," *Wall Street Journal*, January 13, 2016, https://www .wsj.com/articles/chocolate-makers-fight-a-melting-supply-of -cocoa-1452738616.

11. Laura Hennessey Martens, "Darden School, APCO Worldwide Team Up to Rank World's 'Top 100 Champion Brands,'" *UVA Today*, November 12, 2014, https://news.virginia.edu/content /darden-school-apco-worldwide-team-rank-world-s-top -100-champion-brands.

12. Mihai Andrei, "Why Nestle Is One of the Most Hated Companies in the World," *ZME Science*, last modified May 19, 2017, http://www.zmescience.com/science/nestle-company -pollution-children/.

13. "Nestlé boycott successes," babymilkaction.org, accessed July 17, 2017, http://www.babymilkaction.org/nestle-boycott-successes.

14. Rose Hackman, "Nestle Bottled Water Operations Spark Protests Amid California Drought," *The Guardian*, May 20, 2015, https://www.theguardian.com/us-news/2015/may/20/nestle -water-bottling-california-drought.

15. Charley Cameron, "How Nestle Is Pillaging California Water in the Fourth Year of the State's Worst Drought," *Inhabitat*, May 17, 2015, http://inhabitat.com/how-nestle-is-pillaging-californias -water-in-the-4th-year-of-the-states-worst-drought/.

16. Erwin Wagenhofer, *We Feed the World*, directed by Erwin Wagenhofer (2005; Vienna, Austria: Allegrofilm-Produktions GmbH).

17. George McGraw, "Nestlé Chairman Peter Brabeck Says We Don't Have a Right to Water, Believes We Do Have a Right to Water and Everyone's Confused," April 25, 2013, *Huffington*

Post, http://www.huffingtonpost.com/george-mcgraw/nestle
-chairman-peter-brabeck-water_b_3150150.html.

18. Tim Brown, interview by Matt Dangelantonio, *AirTalk*, KPCC Radio, Pasadena, California, May 14, 2015.

19. Andrei, "Why Nestle Is One of the Most Hated Companies in the World."

20. Kate Taylor, "People Are Furious at Nestlé for 'Rape' of Michigan Water Source 120 Miles from Flint," *Business Insider*, November 7, 2016, http://www.businessinsider.com/nestle-expands-michigan -water-plant-2016-11.

21. Erika Fry, "Nestle's Half-Billion-Dollar Noodle Debacle in India," *Fortune*, April 26, 2016, http://fortune.com/nestle-maggi-noodle -crisis/.

22. Amy Mitchell, Jeffrey Gottfried, Michael Barthel, and Elsa Shearer, "The Modern News Consumer: News Attitudes and Practices in the Digital Era," *Pew Research Center*, July 7, 2016, http:// www.journalism.org/2016/07/07/the-modern-news-consumer/.

23. Barie Carmichael, "Inherent Negatives: Reputation Through the Windshield, Not the Rearview Mirror," *APCO Forum*, March 22, 2017, http://apcoworldwide.com/blog/detail/apcoforum/2017 /03/22/inherent-negatives-managing-reputation-through-the -windshield-not-the-rearview-mirror.

24. Henry Mintzberg, *Mintzberg on Management: Inside Our Strange World of Organizations* (New York: Free Press, 1990); Henry Mintzberg, "The Manager's Job: Folklore and Fact," *Harvard Business Review*, March–April 1990, https://hbr.org /1990/03/the-managers-job-folklore-and-fact.

25. Barie Carmichael and James Rubin, "Dow Corning—A New Model for Crisis Management," *Strategic Communication Management*, December/January 2002.

26. For more information, see the Council's website, http://www .dow.com/en-us/science-and-sustainability/collaborations /sustainability-external-advisory-council.

27. Robert Reiss, "Saving the Planet While Generating Profit," *Forbes*, May 3, 2010, https://www.forbes.com/2010/05/03/david-steiner -waste-management-leadership-managing-reiss.html.
28. Jack Witthaus, "This Is Waste Management's Biggest Challenge, New CEO Says," Jack Witthaus, *Houston Business Journal*, November 17, 2016, http://www.bizjournals.com/houston/news /2016/11/17/this-is-waste-managements-biggest-challenge -new.html.
29. Leon Kaye, "UPS CSR Report: Shipping More, Emitting Less," *Triple Pundit*, July 30, 2013, http://www.triplepundit.com/2013 /07/ups-csr-report-2012/.
30. "ORION Backgrounder," www.pressroom.ups.com.
31. Leon Kaye, "UPS CSR Report."
32. Geoff Colvin, "Why Facebook Can't Stop the Fake News," *Fortune*, November 21, 2016, http://fortune.com/2016/11/21 /facebook-zuckerberg-fake-news-stop/.
33. Olivia Solon, "Facebook's Failure: Did Fake News and Polarized Politics Get Trump Elected?," *The Guardian*, November 10, 2016, https://www.theguardian.com/technology/2016/nov/10 /facebook-fake-news-election-conspiracy-theories.
34. Abby Ohlheiser, "This Is How Facebook's Fake-News Writers Make Money," *Washington Post*, November 18, 2016, https:// www.washingtonpost.com/news/the-intersect/wp/2016/11/18 /this-is-how-the-internets-fake-news-writers-make-money/?utm _term=.27e5fa37cdf1.
35. Alexander Smith and Vladimir Banic, "Fake News: How a Partying Macedonian Teen Earns Thousands Publishing Lies," *NBC News*, December 9, 2016, http://www.nbcnews.com/news/world /fake-news-how-partying-macedonian-teen-earns-thousands -publishing-lies-n692451.
36. Casey Newton, Twitter post, November 10, 2016, 9:55 PM, https://twitter.com/caseynewton/status/796909159174127616 ?lang=en.
37. Colvin, "Why Facebook Can't Stop the Fake News."

38. Adam Mosseri, "Working to Stop Misinformation and False News," April 6, 2017, newsroom.fb.com, https://newsroom.fb.com/news /2017/04/working-to-stop-misinformation-and-false-news/.

39. Associated Press, "Google to Ban Fake News Sites from Its Advertising Network," *Los Angeles Times*, November 14, 2016, http:// www.latimes.com/business/technology/la-fi-tn-google-fake -news-20161114-story.html.

40. Colvin, "Why Facebook Can't Stop the Fake News."

41. *The Business Case for the Green Economy: Sustainable Return on Investment*, United Nations Environment Programme, 2012, p. 7 (emphasis added).

42. Gilbert S. Hedstrom, "Director Notes: Navigating the Sustainability Transformation," Number DN-V7N1, *The Conference Board*, January 2015.

43. Coca-Cola Company, "Responsible Water Management in India and Beyond," coca-colacompany.com, February 15, 2016, http://www.coca-colacompany.com/stories/responsible-water -management-in-india-and-beyond.

44. Ibid.

45. "Diageo Marketing Code," Diageo, February 1, 2016, https://www .drinkiq.com/en-ca/resources/diageo-marketing-code-dmc/.

46. Diageo, "Press Release: Diageo Unveils Immersive Virtual Reality that Puts Consumers in the Front Seat of a Collision," *PR Newswire*, November 17, 2016, http://www.prnewswire.com /news-releases/diageo-unveils-immersive-virtual-reality -technology-that-puts-consumers-in-front-seat-of-a-drunk -driving-collision-300365037.html.

47. Jamie Gregora, "Germany Threatens Facebook with Criminal Action for 'Hate Speech' Violations," *The Daily Signal*, October 20, 2016, http://dailysignal.com/2016/10/20/germany-threatens -facebook-with-criminal-action-for-hate-speech-violations/.

48. Chauncey L. Alcorn, "How Facebook Is Revamping Its Fight to End Online Hate Speech," *Fortune*, September 22, 2016, http:// fortune.com/2016/09/22/facebook-hate-speech/.

49. Klint Finley, "Twitter Is Adding New Filtering Tools in an Effort to Curb Abuse," *Wired*, November 15, 2016, https://www.wired.com/2016/11/twitter-adding-new-filtering-tools-effort-curb-abuse/.

4. CORPORATE CHARACTER

1. Jena McGregor, "This IBM Employee Quit Over Her CEO's Letter to Donald Trump," *Washington Post*, November 29, 2016, https://www.washingtonpost.com/news/on-leadership/wp/2016/11/29/this-ibm-employee-quit-over-her-ceos-letter-to-donald-trump-2/?utm_term=.b7463142ff26.
2. Judie Bort, "This Is How Angry Some IBM and Oracle Employees Are Because Their CEOs Are Working with Trump," *Business Insider*, December 20, 2016, http://www.businessinsider.com/employees-at-ibm-oracle-angry-over-trump-2016-12.
3. Wally Olins, *The Brand Handbook* (London: Thames and Hudson, 2008).
4. Kim Bhasin, "L.L. Bean's Duck Boot Finally Gets a Fresh Look," April 7, 2017. Bloomberg, https://www.bloomberg.com/news/articles/2017-04-07/l-l-bean-s-duck-boot-finally-gets-a-fresh-look.
5. Wally Olins, *On Brand* (London: Thames and Hudson, 2003).
6. Mike McPhate, "Whole Foods Says Customer Faked Anti-gay Cake Slur," *New York Times*, April 16, 2016, https://www.nytimes.com/2016/04/22/business/whole-foods-says-customer-faked-anti-gay-cake-slur.html.
7. Majken Schultz and Mary Jo Hatch, "A European View on Corporate Identity: An Interview with Wally Olins," *Journal of Management Inquiry* 6, no. 4 (1997): 330–39.
8. Zoe Thomas, "David Abney: The UPS Boss Who Rose from the Bottom Rung," *BBC News*, August 22, 2016, http://www.bbc.co.uk/news/business-37087358.
9. Sheera Frenkel, "Renegade Facebook Employees Form Task Force to Battle Fake News," *BuzzFeed*, November 14, 2016,

https://www.buzzfeed.com/sheerafrenkel/renegade-facebook
-employees-form-task-force-to-battle-fake-n?utm_term
=.nd8yzKKOn#.jh83Pllyj.

10. Madeline Farber, "Google Tops Apple as the World's Most Valuable Brand," *Fortune*, February 2, 2017, http://fortune.com
/2017/02/02/google-tops-apple-brand-value/.

11. Richard Frye, "Millennials Surpass Gen Xers as Largest Generation in the American Labor Force," pewresearch.org, May 11, 2015.

12. Jeff Wilser, "Dialing Up," *Comstock*, February 28, 2017, https://
www.comstocksmag.com/longreads/dialing.

13. "The 2016 Deloitte Millennial Survey. Winning Over the Next
Generation of Leaders," https://deloittelibrary.com.cy/hotnews
/millennial-survey-2016, accessed July 18, 2017; https://www2
.deloitte.com/content/dam/Deloitte/global/Documents
/About-Deloitte/gx-millenial-survey-2016-exec-summary.pdf.

14. Marlene S. Neill, "Trends in Internal Communication: Genera-
tional Shifts, Internal Social Media and Engagement," *Institute
for Public Relations*, March 1, 2016, http://www.instituteforpr
.org/trends-in-internal-communication-generational-shifts
-internal-social-media-engagement/.

15. Associated Press, "Millennials Earn 20 Percent Less than Boomers Did at Same Stage of Life," *USA Today*, January 13, 2016,
https://www.usatoday.com/story/money/2017/01/13
/millennials-falling-behind-boomer-parents/96530338/.

16. "Starbucks College Achievement Plan," Starbucks, https://
www.starbucks.com/careers/college-plan, access July 17, 2017.

17. Hope King, "Boxed CEO Pays for His Workers' Kids' College
Tuition," *CNN Tech*, June 12, 2015, http://money.cnn.com/2015
/06/12/technology/boxed-ceo-pays-college-tuitions/index
.html.

18. Julie Beck, "How Legos Became More Violent," *The Atlantic*,
May 25, 2016, https://www.theatlantic.com/technology/archive
/2016/05/how-legos-got-more-violent/484286/. The nuanced
distinction was missed by many online articles and comments,

whose writers were surprised by the incongruity between what was understood to be Lego's corporate character and its evolving product strategies.

19. Brian Clark Howard, "I Never Get Tired of Looking at It," *Daily Mail*, June 16, 2011.
20. "The Novo Nordisk Way," Novo Nordisk, http://www .novonordisk.com/about-novo-nordisk/novo-nordisk-way .html, accessed July 20, 2017.
21. Dana Brown and Jette Steen Knudsen, "Director Notes: Generating Value for Investors and Society," Number DN-V5N15, *The Conference Board*, August 2013.
22. "Patagonia: Don't Buy Our Jackets, Fix the Old Ones!" *Recycling Point*, December 8, 2015, http://www.recyclingpoint.info /patagonia-dont-buy-our-jackets-fix-the-old-ones/?lang=en.

5. THE NEW CORPORATE BRANDING

1. Erin Griffith, "Selling Stuff Is No Longer the Point of Retail Stores," Fortune.com, June 8. 2017, http://fortune.com/2017 /06/08/retail-stores-brand-experiences/.
2. Mary Jo Hatch and Majken Schultz, "Are the Stratgic Stars Aligned for Your Corporate Brand?," *Harvard Business Review*, February 2001, https://hbr.org/2001/02/are-the-strategic-stars -aligned-for-your-corporate-brand.
3. Jack Marshall, "The Graphic Shows Why Google Got Into Trouble Over Ad Placement," *Wall Street Journal*, March 23, 2017, https://www.wsj.com/articles/this-graphic-shows-why -google-got-in-trouble-over-ad-placement-1490295628.
4. Kimberly Adams, "The High Price of North Carolina's Transgender Bathroom Bill," *Marketplace*, March 9, 2016, https://www .marketplace.org/2016/05/09/business/north-carolina -transgender-bathroom-bill-comes-cost.
5. Chuck Lindell, "200 Texas Small Businesses Oppose Transgender Bathroom Law," *Statesman*, October 25, 2016, http://www

.statesman.com/news/200-texas-small-businesses-oppose
-transgender-bathroom-law/4oazo19dGQhXh0
EWlRUTQM/.

6. Daniel Victor, "Trump Tweet About L.L.Bean Underscores Potential Danger for Brands," *New York Times*, January 12, 2017, https://www.nytimes.com/2017/01/12/us/politics/linda-bean -ll-bean-boycott.html.

7. Katie Mettler, "We Live in Crazy Times: Neo-Nazis Have Declared New Balance the 'Official Shoes of White People,'" *Washington Post*, November 15, 2016, https://www.washingtonpost .com/news/morning-mix/wp/2016/11/15/the-crazy-reason -neo-nazis-have-declared-new-balance-the-official-shoes-of -white-people/?utm_term=.7fa43c4d7d51.

8. Suntae Kim, Matthew J. Karlesky, Christopher G. Myers, and Todd Schifeling, "Why Companies Are Becoming B Corporations," *Harvard Business Review*, June 17, 2016, https://hbr.org/2016 /06/why-companies-are-becoming-b-corporations.

9. "Patagonia Becomes a California Benefit Corporation," January 3, 2012, https://www.treehugger.com/corporate-responsibility /patagonia-becomes-california-benefit-corporation.html.

10. "DanoneWave Established as US' Largest Public Benefit Corporation," April 28, 2017, http://www.sustainablebrands.com /news_and_views/product_innovation/sustainable_brands /danonewave_established_us_largest_public_benefi.

11. James Rubin, Brian Moriarty, and Alison Mehlsak, "Sustainability at the Coca-Cola Company in a New Era of Brand Building," Case Reference Number UVA-BC-0262 (Charlottesville, VA: Darden Business Publishing, 2015). Note: Unless otherwise stated, all material on Coca-Cola in this chapter has been sourced from this case study.

12. Mackenzie Anderson, "Great Things Come in Innovative Packaging: An Introduction to PlantBottle Packaging," http://www .coca-colacompany.com/stories/great-things-come-in-innovative -packaging-an-introduction-to-plantbottle-packaging.

13. "Pepsi Pledges to Slash Sugar," *Food and Drink Business*, October 19, 2016, http://www.foodanddrinkbusiness.com.au/news/pepsico-pledges-to-slash-sugar.
14. Ibid.
15. Jo Confino, "Unilever's Paul Polman: Challenging the Corporate Status Quo," *Guardian*, April 24, 2012, https://www.theguardian.com/sustainable-business/paul-polman-unilever-sustainable-living-plan.
16. Unilever, "Targets and Performance," https://www.unilever.com/sustainable-living/reducing-environmental-impact/sustainable-sourcing/#244-502893, accessed July 18, 2017.
17. "Unilever: In Search of the Good Business," *Economist*, August 9, 2014, http://www.economist.com/news/business/21611103-second-time-its-120-year-history-unilever-trying-redefine-what-it-means-be.
18. Christopher Cole, "Unilever Settles Hair Loss Class a Action for $10M," findlaw.com, March 28, 2016, http://blogs.findlaw.com/decided/2016/03/unilever-settles-hair-loss-class-action-for-10m.html.
19. "Innovating to Reduce Greenhouse Gases," Unilever, https://www.unilever.com/sustainable-living/the-sustainable-living-plan/reducing-environmental-impact/greenhouse-gases/innovating-solutions-to-reduce-greenhouse-gases, accessed July 17, 2017.
20. "Unilever's Sustainable Living Brands Continue to Drive Higher Rates of Growth," May 18, 2017, https://www.unilever.com/news/Press-releases/2017/unilevers-sustainable-living-brands-continue-to-drive-higher-rates-of-growth.html.
21. "The 2016 Sustainability Leaders: A GlobeScan/SustainAbility Survey," *GlobeScan*, June 7, 2016, http://www.globescan.com/component/edocman/?view=document&id=250&Itemid=591.
22. "How Companies Can Tap Sustainability to Motivate Staff," *Knowledge@Wharton*, September 29, 2016, http://knowledge

.wharton.upenn.edu/article/how-companies-tap-sustainability
-to-motivate-staff/.

23. Associated Press, "Volkswagen to Shed 30,000 Jobs to Cut
Costs After Emissions-Cheating Scandal," *Los Angeles Times,*
November 18, 2016, http://www.latimes.com/business/la-fi-hy
-volkswagen-job-cuts-20161118-story.html.

24. Joseph Schumpeter, "Call the B Team," *Economist,* October 6,
2012, http://economist.com/node/21564197.

25. Jo Confino, "Richard Branson and Jochen Zeitz launch B Team
challenge," *Guardian,* June 13, 2013, https://www.theguardian.
com/sustainable-business/blog/richard-branson-jochen-zeitz
-b-team.

26. N. Craig Smith, "When It Comes to CSR, Size Matters," *Forbes,*
August 14, 2013.

27. Fran Hawthorne, "Socially Responsible Small Businesses Often
Grow Very Large," entrepreneur.com, June 16, 2015, https://
www.entrepreneur.com/article/247339.

28. bthechange.com, "Happy Family's Shazi Visram and Danone's
Lorna Davis on How Going Big Doesn't Have to Mean Selling
Out," December 7, 2016, https://bthechange.com/happy-familys
-shazi-visram-and-danone-s-lorna-davis-on-how-going-big
-doesn-t-have-to-mean-selling-132f5fdc409e.

29. Ibid.

30. bcorporation.net, "Danone Joins Multinational Advisory
Council," January 7, 2016, https://www.bcorporation.net/blog
/danone-joins-multinational-advisory-council.

31. Hamdi Ulukaya, "Chobani's Founder on Growing a Start-Up
Without Outside Investors," *Harvard Business Review,* October
2013.

32. Yuki Noguchi, "Why Chobani Gave Employees a Financial Stake
in the Company," NPR, *All Things Considered,* April 28, 2016,
http://www.npr.org/sections/thesalt/2016/04/28/476021520
/why-chobani-gave-employees-a-financial-stake-in-companys
-future.

6. REPUTATION LOST AND FOUND

1. "How Online Reviews Have Been a Blessing for Travelers and a Curse for Some Big Hotels," Marketwatch, May 16, 2017, http://www.marketwatch.com/story/big-hotels-are-losing-their-edge-thanks-to-online-reviews-2017-05-16?.
2. Michael Hiltzik, "Wells Fargo Scandal Report Details Board of Directors Dereliction of Duty, But Gives Them a Pass," *Los Angeles Times*, April 10, 2017, http://www.latimes.com/business/hiltzik/la-fi-hiltzik-wells-board-20170410-story.html.
3. Barbara Carmichael and James Rubin, "Aetna Inc.: Managing Inherent Enterprise Risks through Stakeholder Management," Case Reference Number UCA-SB-0218, (Charlottesville, VA: Darden Business Publishing, 2009). Note: The Aetna example used in this chapter is based on this published case study.
4. Barie Carmichael and James Rubin, "Dow Corning—A New Model for Crisis Management," *Strategic Communications Management* 6, no. 1 (2001): 22–25.
5. Roger Bolton, "Restoring Public Trust in Business: Emerging Opportunities for Leaders," (presentation, Arthur W. Page Society, Baruch College, City University of New York, New York, NY, September 23, 2009).
6. Rubin and Carmichael, "Aetna Inc."
7. Ibid.
8. Bolton, "Restoring Public Trust in Business."
9. More than a decade after Dow Corning's 2002 permanent withdrawal from the breast implant market, in 2017 the FDA reported a new possible link between saline or silicone gel implants having a textured surface and a rare form of lymphoma which was not an issue during the 1990s controversy. U.S. Food and Drug Administration, "Breast Implant-Associated Anaplastic Large Cell Lymphoma (BIA-ALCL)," https://www.fda.gov/MedicalDevices/ProductsandMedicalProcedures/ImplantsandProsthetics/BreastImplants/ucm239995.htm, accessed July 18, 2017.

10. "Chronology of Silicone Breast Implants," *PBS Frontline*, http://www.pbs.org/wgbh/pages/frontline/implants/chron.html, accessed July 17, 2017.

11. Lilly Workneh, "Jesse Williams Wants You to 'Stay Woke'" in the New Film on Black Lives Matter," *Huffington Post*, May 16, 2016, http://www.huffingtonpost.com/entry/jesse-williams-stay-woke-documentary-black-lives-matter_us_5739516ee4b077d4d6f3688a.

12. Laurel Wamsley, "After Uproar, Pepsi Halts Rollout of Controversial Protest-Themed Ad," *NPR*, April 5, 2017, http://www.npr.org/sections/thetwo-way/2017/04/05/522750764/after-uproar-pepsi-halts-rollout-of-controversial-protest-themed-ad.

13. Eli Blumenthal, "The Scene at JFK as Taxi Drivers Strike Following Trump's Immigration Ban," *USA Today*, January 29, 2017, https://www.usatoday.com/story/news/2017/01/28/taxi-drivers-strike-jfk-airport-following-trumps-immigration-ban/97198818/.

14. Patrick Sisson, "How Uber and Lyft Responded to a Taxi Strike at JFK Airport," Curbed, February 1, 2017, www.curbed.com https://www.curbed.com/2017/1/29/14430070/taxi-uber-lyft-jfk-airport-protest.

15. Ibid.

16. Henry Grabar, "The Uber Boycott and Lyft's ACLU Donation Herald a New Era of Corporate Politics," *Slate*, January 30, 2017, http://www.slate.com/blogs/moneybox/2017/01/30/the_uber_boycott_and_lyft_s_aclu_donation_herald_a_new_era_of_corporate.html.

7. RESETTING THE SWEET SPOT

1. Nik Gowing and Chris Langdon, *Thinking the Unthinkable: A New Imperative for Leadership in the Digital Age* (London: Chartered Institute of Management Accountants, 2016), http://www.thinkunthinkable.org/.

2. BCBS press release, "Blue Cross and Blue Shield and Lyft Join Forces to Increase Access to Health Care in Communities with Transportation Deserts," May 10, 2017, https://www.bcbs.com /news/press-releases/blue-cross-and-blue-shield-and-lyft-join -forces-increase-access-health-care, accessed 7.18.17.

3. Julia Horowitz, "Blue Cross Blue Shield Wants You to Make It to Your Doctor's Appointments—So Much That It's Willing to Pay for Your Lyft," CNN, May 10, 2017, http://money.cnn .com/2017/05/10/technology/lyft-rides-blue-cross-blue -shield/index.html.

4. Lauren Thomas, "United CEO Says Airline Had to 'Re-Accommodate' Passenger, and the Reaction Was Wild," April 10, 2017, CNBC, http://www.cnbc.com/2017/04/10/united-ceo-says -airline-had-to-re-accommodate-passenger-and-twitter-is -having-a-riot.html.

5. Om Malik, "Silicon Valley Has an Empathy Vacuum," *New Yorker*, November 28, 2016, http://www.newyorker.com/business /currency/silicon-valley-has-an-empathy-vacuum.

6. Gowing and Langdon, *Thinking the Unthinkable*.

7. Pavan Sukhdev, *Corporation 2020: Transforming Business for Tomorrow's World*, (Washington, DC: Island Press, 2012).

8. Andy Grove, "Andy Grove: How America Can Create Jobs," *Bloomberg Businessweek*, July 1, 2010, https://www.bloomberg .com/news/articles/2010-07-01/andy-grove-how-america -can-create-jobs.

9. Muhtar Kent, "Opinion: The Golden Triangle—Spearheading Change the Smart Way," November 7, 2012, http://www.coca -colacompany.com/stories/opinion-the-golden-triangle -spearheading-change-the-smart-way.

10. Sustainable Brands, "CEOs of 30 More Major US Brands Pen Letter to Trump, Urging Adherence to Paris Agreement," sustainablebrands.com, May 16, 2017.

11. Lauren Etter and Shruti Singh, "Big Meat Braces for Refugee Shortage," *Bloomberg Businessweek*, February 8, 2017, https://

www.bloomberg.com/news/articles/2017-02-09/big-meat-braces-for-a-refugee-shortage.

12. Caitlin Dewey, "The One Piece of Michelle Obama's Legacy That President Trump Can't Wreck," *Washington Post*, May 11, 2017, https://www.washingtonpost.com/news/wonk/wp/2017/05/11/the-one-piece-of-michelle-obamas-legacy-that-president-trump-cant-wreck/?utm_term=.5e7773f67239.

13. Charles Duhigg and Keith Bradsher, "Apple, America and a Squeezed Middle Class, " *New York Times*, January 11, 2012, http://www.nytimes.com/2012/01/22/business/apple-america-and-a-squeezed-middle-class.html.

14. Elizabeth Gurdus, "Exclusive: Apple Just Promised to Give US Manufacturing a $1 Billion Boost," May 3, 2017, CNBC, http://www.cnbc.com/2017/05/03/exclusive-apple-just-promised-to-give-us-manufacturing-a-1-billion-boost.html.

15. Mark Egan, "Ecomagination Ten Years Later: Proving the Efficiency and Economics Go Hand-in-Hand," *GE Reports: Sustainability*, November 29, 2015, http://www.gereports.com/ecomagination-ten-years-later-proving-efficiency-economics-go-hand-hand/.

16. Allan Murray, "GE's Immelt Signals End to 7 Decades of Globalization," *Fortune*, May 20, 2016, http://fortune.com/2016/05/20/ge-immelt-globalization/.

17. Ibid.

INDEX

INDEX

INDEX